MW01128344

THE FOREX MINDSET

The Skills and Winning Attitude You Need for MORE PROFITABLE FOREX TRADING

Jared F. Martinez

New York Chicago San Francisco Lisbon London Madrid Mexico City
Milan New Delhi San Juan Seoul Singapore Sydney Toronto

Copyright © 2011 by Jared Martinez. All rights reserved. Printed in the United States
of America. Except as permitted under the United States Copyright Act of 1976, no part
of this publication may be reproduced or distributed in any form or by any means, or
stored in a database or retrieval system, without the prior written permission of the
publisher.

1 2 3 4 5 6 7 8 9 10 11 12 13 14 15 16 17   QFR/QFR   1 9 8 7 6 5 4 3 2 1

ISBN 978-0-07-176734-7
MHID   0-07-176734-7

e-ISBN 978-0-07-176736-1
e-MHID   0-07-176736-3

This publication is designed to provide accurate and authoritative information in regard
to the subject matter covered. It is sold with the understanding that neither the author
nor the publisher is engaged in rendering legal, accounting, securities trading, or other
professional services. If legal advice or other expert assistance is required, the services
of a competent professional person should be sought.
  —*From a Declaration of Principles Jointly Adopted by a Committee of the*
  American Bar Association and a Committee of Publishers and Associations

Library of Congress Cataloging-in-Publication Data

Martinez, Jared F.
    The Forex mindset : the skills and winning attitude you need for more profitable
    Forex trading / by Jared Martinez.
        p.   cm.
    ISBN 978-0-07-176734-7 (alk. paper)
    1. Foreign exchange market.   2. Foreign exchange futures.
    3. Speculation—Psychological aspects.   I. Title.

    HG3851.M316   2011
    332.4′5—dc22   2011008766

McGraw-Hill books are available at special quantity discounts to use as premiums and
sales promotions or for use in corporate training programs. To contact a representative,
please e-mail us at bulksales@mcgraw-hill.com.

This book is printed on acid-free paper.

CONTENTS

ACKNOWLEDGMENTS

My six children—Jared, Jacob, Isaac, Rachael, Joshua, Jordan—and my grandson Jeffery have been the shoulders I could lean on when feeling weak or vulnerable, who supplied me with the necessary strength and courage to keep going, keep persisting, and keep believing that nothing is impossible.

I wish to thank adversity—it, too, has been one of my greatest teachers and mentors. No doubt it has been the grinding stone in my life; some days it really grinds me down, but when I apply what I have written in this book, those skills and disciplines really polish me up and allow me to shine.

It is with my sincere appreciation that I bring tribute and give credit to all the people I know or whom I have read about in life who have been blindsided and had to endure hardship. Their stories have helped me figure out how to work through my fears, anxieties, and hardships, turning my scars into stars. Had it not been for the countless people who mustered up the courage to face adversity and then tell or write about it, the world never would have heard their pearls of wisdom.

Next on my list, I wish to thank two amazing business associates who have heavily participated in my emotional and financial success: my sons Isaac and Jacob. It has been their sheer genius (which never ceases to amaze me) along with their business talent that has put Market Traders Institute (MTI) on the worldwide map. Thank you for being the key strategic players MTI so desperately needed.

Further, their capability has allowed me the freedom to write this book.

Next, I wish to thank Suzanne Keator for all her support and for helping to take this project to the very end. Her genius ability with words and the English language has allowed me to articulate on paper what was in my head. Thank you!

Last, I wish to thank all the MTI clients worldwide for having faith and trust in me. Thank you for opening up your homes and hearts to me and my family. Your shared perception of the world, the market, and countless challenging questions have allowed me to widen my perception of the world and market.

In addition, I would like to thank all our staff and worldwide partners at MTI for their dedication, support, and belief in our vision. You not only are great business partners, but also have become some of my best friends.

I am deeply grateful to all the staff at McGraw-Hill who have participated in bringing this book to market. Thank you for believing in me.

I cannot finish my acknowledgments without recognizing my parents—God rest their souls—who never promised days without pain, laughter without sorrow, or sun without rain, but rather instilled in me a belief of being a Mexi-Can instead of a Mexi-Can't. They gave me strength during my dark days, comfort for my fears and tears, and a light that showed the way!

INTRODUCTION

I am your constant companion,
I am your greatest helper or your heaviest burden.
I will push you onward or drag you down to failure.
I am at your command.

Half of the tasks that you do you might just as well
Turn over to me, and I will do them quickly and correctly.

I am easily managed. You must merely be firm with me.
Show me exactly how you want something done.
After a few lessons, I will do it automatically.

I am the servant of all great people
And the regret of all failures as well.
Those who are great, I have made great.
Those who are failures, I have made failures.

I am not a machine, but I will work with all its precision
Plus the intelligence of a person.

Now you may run me for profit, or you may run me for ruin.
It makes no difference to me.

Take me, train me, be firm with me, and
I will lay the world at your feet.
Be easy with me, and I will destroy you.
I am called Habit!

—Author Unknown

Due to my commitment to students, my sister gave this poem about habit six months before she passed away from cancer. She asked me to share it with everyone I taught and who was trying to chase a dream, trying to reach their highest potential at becoming a successful Forex trader! She said I should ask each student who wants to become a Forex trader, "So you want to become a Forex trader? Tell me what your habits are, and I will tell you if you have a fighting chance!" So I ask, what are your habits?

Emotion Versus Skill

It took me well over 10 years to discover that in trading, 10 percent is skill and technique while 90 percent is having the right mindset to acquire the necessary habits for managing your emotions. I founded the Market Traders Institute (MTI) in 1994 and have since been involved in training more than 10,000 clients worldwide on how to trade the Forex. I have discovered that the journey all these students embark on is completely different than the journey they end up taking. They start their journey learning the technical skills and techniques of successful trading, yet they quickly realize that emotional intelligence, self-awareness, and the discovery of their mental abilities in times of trading stress or financial crisis become the major component of achieving their financial goal. Simply said, they realize their mindset is the key to their success.

A Quick Introduction to the Forex

Forex is an acronym for *For*eign *Ex*change, which is also known as the cash market or spot interbank market. In the market, which was established in 1971, people exchange one country's currency for another country's currency. The spot market means trading right on the spot at whatever the price is at the moment of the transaction. The Forex market is the arena where the currencies of countries are exchanged for another to do business internationally. Payments for import and export purchases and sales of goods or services between countries all flow through the foreign exchange market.

The Forex market is considered the largest financial market in the world. More than 3.5 trillion dollars is traded on the Forex per day. Three hundred billion dollars a day is traded on the U.S. Treasury bond market, and 100 billion dollars is traded on the U.S. stock market every day it is open, totaling 400 billion dollars per day. The Forex trades over eight times that volume and equals more than all the combined world financial markets.

The Forex marketplace has no physical location; it is an electronic medium where transactions are placed automatically through the Internet, squawk boxes, or via telephone. Approximately 4,500 world banks and retail brokers all watch the current prices constantly change and execute transactions for clients. Small individual traders wanting to capture profit by speculating on price changes gain access to the market through a Forex broker. Traders receive their financial reward in a measurement called pips (price interest points), normally expressed in decimals, which are then converted into dollars.

Trading on the Forex is considered the ultimate financial as well as mind game for traders, mainly due to the incredible instant financial rewards as well as losses.

Building the Right Mindset for Success

Markets are driven by greed and fear. We get into the markets out of greed and get out due to fear. As fear is based on something that we think may happen in the future, it is clearly a mental process that tries to predict the future—in that sense, the reason for the fear is a projection of our mind. We can be afraid to fall, but once we are falling, we are afraid to hit the ground. Once we hit the ground, we may fear we are badly injured. Once we know we are badly injured, we may fear the pain and consequences of not being able to work for some time or becoming disabled. So one could say that fear is always based on something that has not happened yet and is therefore a fantasy of our mind rather than fact.

Most traders jump in the markets out of greed and end up on one of the worst adventures of their lives. This self-inflicted process results from their lack of education, emotional intelligence, and ability to control their emotions in times of financial crisis. The average person does not know how to properly think while in a state of stress or fear. The dream journey they embarked on can turn into a life-altering nightmare.

Is it any wonder that with the financial markets so heavily driven by greed and fear, with the average trader knowing nothing about the subject of greed or fear, that many traders find themselves heading down a path of self-destruction, experiencing a sort of financial death due to their ignorance of the market?

Learning how to handle your emotions while trading will lead to incredible self-awareness. Why? Your past reaches into your present and programs your future. When you trade, you bring all your bad emotional habits and actions to the trading table and subconsciously apply them. When you choose a behavior, you choose a consequence. We are all nothing more than the choices we make.

Change is difficult if not impossible for some. If you want to make it as a trader, you must change all those bad habits that have kept you in a state of managing your poverty or mediocrity in your life. You must change, replacing bad, destructive habits with constructive and productive, good life habits. If you don't, you will discover that when it comes to trading, you will not reach your greatest potential or learn that trading knowledge and emotional intelligence are the keys that keep you free from financial incarceration.

Most people fear success. They specifically fear financial success. If they are unsuccessful in this part of their lives, they often-times find someone to blame it on, someone who is responsible, someone holding them down or taking their opportunities away.

As long as they have a scapegoat in their lives, they feel they are not responsible for their actions. But the moment they start to incur financial success, they then have to take on the responsibility for themselves and their achievements: that scares most people to death.

In life, as well as in trading, nothing is to be feared; it is only to be understood. As you read this book, you will be challenged to purge yourself of your bad habits. You will be shown how in this life we are our worst enemies and the ones who stand in the way of experiencing the financial success we have always dreamed of. Just as in trading, true success in life is 90 percent emotional intelligence and 10 percent skill (the complete opposite of what everyone thinks).

Every dream is in the mind of the believer and in the hands of the doer. We are not given dreams without being given the power to make them come true. There are attainable keys to making dreams come true—you just need to discover what they are and learn the appropriate necessary skills.

If you are not making the money in your life that you always dreamed of, perhaps it is because you are locked into a series of unproductive work habits and destructive mindsets. Perhaps you have created a mental block inside you that has stopped you from earning more than you think you are worth. If you want to earn more than you are earning right now, you must upgrade your self-concept.

The knowledge contained in this book will help you pursue your dreams as a successful trader. For you cannot dream yourself into a position of a successful trader; you must work your way into it, and you must take on the responsibility of your destination just as I have done mine. You must believe you can achieve your dream. The things we truly believe in always happen, because it is this belief that makes it happen.

So the real question remains, how badly do you want it? Do you want it badly enough to be willing to sacrifice who you are for who you may become? After watching many people self-destruct and others make wealth beyond their belief, I have learned that success in trading requires only an open mind, humility, commitment, a true willingness to improve your life via change, and sheer persistence. Because in the confrontation between the river and the rock, the river always wins—not through strength, but through persistence. Look at the Grand Canyon!

CHAPTER 1

GET EXCITED ABOUT TRADING

You have a gold mine when you have a goal in mind.

More than likely, the reason you bought this book is because when you heard how the Forex works, you started to dream about becoming a successful trader. You were excited about the prospects of how great it would be to succeed at something very few others have. There is nothing better than a dream to get you motivated or on the road to success, but as with any dream, it is important to maintain your sense of excitement. Nothing great happens unless you set a goal or start to dream. Think about it: most people are not in the habit of doing either, and they instead simply exist, day-to-day, with no real quest for achievement. If you've lost excitement in your goals and dreams, it's time to reenergize and get it back, or find new ones to strive for.

To reach your fullest potential at anything, you need to get excited about what you are doing and where you are going. The majority of the world gets up day in and day out, going to work doing something they really don't enjoy or want to do. As Henry David Thoreau wrote in 1854, "The mass of men lead lives of quiet desperation." Are you one of the fortunate few who jump out of bed with excitement ready to start your day and looking forward to all the opportunities for success that will be knocking on your door? Or are you one of the masses who fall out of bed and begrudgingly get up to start another day of quiet desperation? Consider the following about people today:

- We have higher buildings and wider highways but shorter temperaments and narrower points of view.
- We spend more but enjoy less.
- We have bigger houses but smaller families.
- We have more commitments but less time.
- We have more knowledge but less judgment.
- We have more medicines but less health.
- We have multiplied our possessions but reduced our values.
- We talk much, we love only a little, and we hate too much.
- We reached the moon and came back, but we find it troublesome to cross our own street and meet our neighbors.
- We have conquered outer space, but not our inner space.
- We have higher income but fewer morals.
- We bring home two salaries but have more divorces.
- We have more liberty but less joy.
- We have more food but less nutrition.
- We have finer houses but more broken homes.

Although no one can go back and make a brand new start, anyone can start now and make a brand new ending:

- Don't wait for that special moment in time. Make it.
- Don't wait for the special road of opportunity to open up. Go create it.
- Don't wait for money to appear. Go earn it.
- Don't go for less. Go for the best.
- Don't back down. Go around.
- Don't close your eyes. Open your mind.
- Don't avoid or be afraid of failure. Learn to use it to your advantage.
- Don't fight your misfortune. Transform it, and make a fortune.
- Don't worry about your mistakes. Everyone makes them.
- Don't let how you feel make you forget what you deserve.
- Don't compare. Just be aware.

- Don't wait for love. Go find it, feel it, and give it.
- Don't run from what life has to offer.

Spread your wings—you have no idea how far you can truly fly when you have a dream or a goal!

Follow Your Dreams

There is nothing like a dream or a goal to get you excited and motivated about your future. Dreams and goals are necessary in life, but as I say at the beginning of every mentorship class I teach: "You cannot dream yourself into a position of a successful trader. You must work your way into it. You must take on the responsibility of your destination as I have done mine. You must believe you can achieve it. The things we believe in will always happen, because it is the belief in those things that will make it happen. Remember, if another person can do it, *you* can do it."

You have to figure out the skills and disciplines needed to fulfill your dream. Then buckle down and do it, with the belief that whatever you expect, you will get. I have learned that a dream combined with an expectation and the courage to pursue it make it a reality. The poorest of all people is not a person without a cent, but a person without a dream!

> The poorest of all people is not a person without
> a cent, but a person without a dream!

When you are involved with doing what you dream about, something that truly excites you, you dig deep into your soul to bring out the very best you have to offer the world. Usually we are so excited about our dream that we begin to tell everyone about it well before we figure out any details about how we are going to accomplish it. Why? First, it's just no fun to dream alone. Second, when we dream alone, it's unlikely our dream will ever become a reality. When we dream with others, it's the beginning of a new life, a new road, a new future. When people vocalize their dreams, they provide an intimate look into their heart and character. As long as we are still alive and breathing, we owe it to ourselves to never give up chasing our dreams.

Continuing Your Education

Every dream is in the mind of the believer and in the hands of the doer. Learning to become a successful currency trader may be your dream, and to attain it you must learn the skills of a Forex trader. You better invest in your education about how this market works, because you will be put up against some of the brightest traders in the world. Learn the skills and traits of a successful trader and replicate them.

If you are not making the money in your life you always dreamed of, perhaps it is because you are locked into a series of unproductive work habits and destructive mindsets. Maybe you have created a mental block inside you that has stopped you from earning more than you think you are worth. If you want to earn more than you are earning right now, you must upgrade your self-concept.

Now that you have found the Forex, you need to begin to identify all the knowledge you need to acquire to become a successful trader and begin to study everything necessary to achieve success as a trader. Knowing as much as you can is important, not because you will use all that information, but because it will give you options.

It is imperative to be committed not only to continued education about your new venture that excites you but also to learning more about your emotions and how to control them instead of letting them control you. If you think your current education is sufficient to take you where you need to go, you're wrong. It doesn't matter if you are starting a restaurant, a retail store, or a service-based business, or if you are becoming a Forex trader: you are going up against some of the brightest people in the world. And if you think you can take them on without any further education, guidance, or mentorship, then you will be in for the surprise of your life. Why? When a person with money goes up against a person with education and experience, after everything is said and done, the person with the education and experience will end up with the money and the person who had the money will end up with the experience.

When we invest in ourselves, we create a lasting asset, as compared to investing in a couch, state-of-the-art stereo system, boat, or credit card debt from buying more stuff, which are all depreciating assets. The average person spends more money on household furniture (a depreciating asset) than on education for work, and then wonders why things aren't improving in his or her personal or financial work life.

> When we invest in ourselves, we are creating a lasting asset.

Your furniture can't make you more money and is not going to increase in value. But over time, investing more in yourself than in your furniture will allow you to buy all the furniture you desire for your house. Depreciating assets can't do that.

Another problem we face in chasing dreams is learning to manage our wants versus our needs. We want a new car, but do we need a $100,000 car, when in reality we can take the difference of perhaps a $30,000 car versus a $100,000 car and invest in more education that perhaps will allow us to buy as many cars as we want? We want a new boat, but we need more money in the bank to earn interest, which would enable our money to work for us so we can buy a new boat down the road with the interest earned. Our thought processes about life and earning income are all screwed up. Believe it or not, if our parents or caregivers went through life with a mindset stemming from poverty or mediocrity, that likely has rubbed off on us. The mindset passed on places us in a position to repeat their bad habits and be just like them, living a life of managing their poverty or mediocrity and doing exactly what they did.

My focus has been to help traders break that spell. Market Traders Institute was created to teach the skills of successful Forex trading as well as the emotional skills for success, enabling traders to have a quantum leap in performance. As you learn more about the Forex, pay attention to the details and train your brain to always pay attention to those details. Successful people are successful for several reasons. Primarily, they pay attention to details. If you want the devil out of your daily work life, pay attention to the details. Choosing not to pay attention to details will only slow you down and invite the devil into your life. Be wary of the person who doesn't notice the details or who gets annoyed when details slow them down. Success and excellence are found in paying attention to the details. So as you read this book, pay attention to the details. It will pay off in huge dividends.

Achieving Balance

Success at anything in life is not a fantasy, it is a formula. Learning how to become a successful trader is a formula, not a fantasy. Part of that formula is living a balanced life. When it comes to trading, all the out-of-balance areas of our lives will have an enhanced effect on our trading.

> Success at anything in life is not a fantasy, it is a formula.

After teaching people how to trade for more than 16 years, I have concluded that to enjoy not only this life but the life of a trader, you must learn to achieve balance in seven major areas of your life:

- Self
- Significant other
- Spiritual

- Family
- Friends
- Work
- Community

I have learned that balance in our lives is a close relative to happiness, and if you are not happy trading, you won't be successful at trading. Many people underestimate how closely tied these seven areas of balance are to our personal happiness and to the success we ultimately enjoy in our professional lives. It may often seem that when one area of your life is out of balance, they all start to get out of balance.

I refer to it as our necessary balance in life. All aspects of our life are important and need to be looked at as a finely tuned, balanced engine. When all the parts are working, the engine can perform at peak performance; however, if parts start to break or wear down, the engine cannot reach peak performance.

Without balance, you can become overly consumed by a certain area of your life, neglecting your needed balance, and eventually frustrated that things are not going well in other areas, which will create bad attitudes and open the door to becoming addicted to negative habits and actions. Like all addictions, they cause additional problems, and in the end you lose. Without self-balance, you become emotionally and physically sick, you lose sight of who you are, and you lose your identity. Without balance in your work, you lose your perspective and your focus on the important aspects of your job, and you begin to perform at substandard levels, opening yourself up to potentially making less money or even losing your job. Without balance in your family, you can lose them. Without balance with your significant other, you can lose him or her. If you lose your significant other and your family, watch the effect it will have on your work environment. You see, who we are is not what we do to make a living. Who we are is a balance of our family, our work, and ourselves—in other words, all the seven areas of our lives that complete our lives.

> Who we are is not what we do to make a living. Who we
> are is a balance of our family, our work, and ourselves.

Any daily frustration that is created by one or more of these components being out of balance will create negative emotional stress. Hold on to it long enough, and you will have created some serious destructive emotional baggage that slowly turns into deep emotional scars and alters your outlook not only on life, but on just about everything you get involved with, even trading.

When you hold on to unproductive emotional baggage from the past, regardless of where it came from, it will stand in the way of your excitement and eventually in achieving the success at trading you are looking for. As a trader, you cannot afford to let that happen. Are you happy and content with where you are in the seven areas of your life that create balance and thus can now live a fulfilled life? Or are you out of balance? If you are out of balance, what are you going to do about it?

Part of happiness is when what you think, how you feel, what you say, and what you do are all in harmony. The wealthiest traders I have met live a life in balance and maintain the necessary harmony needed to become the successes they are. They are usually very kind, generous, and fun, and maintain low profiles in their personal lives. They were human before they became traders, and after all, they still are. Maybe they were somewhat lost before that little seed of a trader's dream was planted deep inside their heart. It was only when they had the courage to water and nurture that seed that this dream came to fruition.

Happiness in Managing Your Success

We are the most advanced and complex organisms on this planet; yet as we begin to work through life, many of us lose our way and begin to malfunction at an early age, both emotionally and financially. Instead of becoming highly productive, fine-tuned, moneymaking (and saving) members of society, we start to live our lives just surviving, living paycheck to paycheck and struggling to get ahead. For some reason we become satisfied to just get by, being unproductive or settling into either a life of poverty or mediocrity. When you live a life of managing your poverty or mediocrity, you lose your direction and purpose. We are here to reach our highest potential at whatever we do. Managing our poverty or mediocrity is not reaching our highest potential. Instead, we need to manage our success.

Too often people attempt to live their lives backward; they try to have more things, more status, more popularity, and more money to do more of what they want so they will be happier. The way life really works is actually in the reverse. You must first be who you really are and then do what you need to do to have what you really want.

I believe that to experience happiness, three key components need to be in play:

- Having something to do that we really enjoy
- Having someone you truly love to share your life
- Having something to always look forward to

Look at the three components of true earthly happiness: are you so excited with what you are doing during your 8 to 10 daily work hours that it is hard to stop? If not, what are you going to do about it? Are you going to keep on keeping on, until one day you look up and say, "Wow, where did my life go?"

I feel sorry for the person who gets up every day unexcited about his work. Not only will he never be satisfied, but he may never achieve anything worthwhile. I feel even sorrier for any person who does not have a dream, because he has a high probability of arriving at retirement age flat broke. And there is nothing happy about that!

Consider component number two for happiness: have you found someone to truly love and share your life, good or bad? If not, why? When it comes time to learn to trade, it sure is comforting when you have a loving companion who believes in you and will support you and your efforts. At the same time, I will tell you, it can be hell if you are living with someone who won't support you or believe in you.

And the last component: Do you get up every day having something to look forward to in your daily or professional life? Do you look forward to going to work or do you look at work as just a price you have to pay to enjoy a great weekend? If you are going to survive as a trader, you need to jump out of bed with all the excitement in the world, looking forward to making more money day in and day out trading.

People are made so that whenever anything ignites their soul, the impossibilities disappear.

For years I dreamed of being a father with lots of kids; today I have lots of kids. Then I started dreaming about becoming a successful trader; and I became a successful trader. Then I dreamed about creating a worldwide company; today, I am the founder of a worldwide company. I can honestly say my list goes on, but this book is not about me—it's about you. So I ask the question: are you still dreaming, or have your dreams all faded away? Trust me, 20 years from now, you will be more disappointed by the dreams you didn't chase than by the ones you did chase. I am so grateful I have not stopped dreaming. The freedom to dream participates in creating happiness. I have learned we are not here on earth for a long time, so we need to be here for a good time and be happy about it, regardless of the obstacles.

Conclusion

The majority of people in the world live in frustration because they cannot acquire the income needed during their work hours to pay for something to look forward to at the end of the week, let alone something like a new car, a new house, an exotic vacation, a new boat, a second home on the beach, and so on. The primary reason they walk around frustrated is they get locked into a subconscious state of managing their poverty or mediocrity instead of success.

It is true that there is a lot of excitement, good and bad, in the journey of life, the thrill of the chase, and in the achievement of goals or dreams; however, with a commitment to continued education about life and your profession, and your personal daily happiness, all that excitement is multiplied a hundredfold.

Learning to become a successful Forex trader can bring back the spark that can ignite your dreams and begin to fund all those things you want to look forward to. I hope you get into the habit of dreaming and setting goals. I hope that whatever dream you start to chase, it places you in a position to dig deep into your soul to bring out the very best in you, enabling you to ultimately achieve that dream.

That's why I propose that as of today—you find your dream, chase it, and live it. We miss 100 percent of the shots we don't take. So I say, get excited and go for it!

CHAPTER 2

FINDING A MENTOR IN TRADING AND IN LIFE

S uccess in life is not a fantasy; it is a formula.
    Find a person with the formula who is experiencing success in the field you wish to pursue, let him mentor you, and you will find your success! A mentor is a person you look up to and respect, a person you want to be like, a person who is an expert in the area you want to sharpen your skills at in your life. If you want to be a better father, go find one whom you admire and who makes you think, "Boy, I would like to be a father to my children just like that!" Then do three things:

- Get to know him.
- Study him.
- Do exactly what he does.

You would do the same thing if you want to be a good spouse, a good friend, or a good trader.

There are more than six billion people on this planet. Just about every person in the world is getting up every day trying to figure out a recipe or formula for their success. Each person is trying to win his or her race, trying to become a winner or champion in his or her own right. The sad part is the majority of the world never really find their niche in life and therefore never reach their highest potential.

Why Find a Mentor?

Only 3 percent of Americans become financially independent by retirement age; 97 percent retire broke.[1] The reality is, for many of us when we left home, Mom and Dad pretty much patted us on the back and said good luck and God bless. They did not hand us a manual for success containing all the instructions or details to live a happy, productive, and financially successful life. No doubt all our parents and caregivers did the best they could, but as the saying goes, sometimes our best isn't good enough. So to succeed, especially financially, we either have to go figure out the formula ourselves (which can be costly and time-consuming), attend college in hopes that we acquire it (though there are many educated derelicts out there), or find a mentor who is willing to help us.

Something magical takes place when you ask someone for help. For some reason, regardless of the situation, human beings just love to help. When you ask people for help, they feel compelled or obligated, or just become willing to help. Either way, when you have the courage to ask for help from a mentor, you have a high percentage chance of receiving guidance.

Now you might be saying to yourself, "Why would a mentor be willing to help me? After all, I might end up becoming the competition." Frankly, if the mentor is worried about that, you need to go find another mentor. After all, truly successful people do not fear competition. Trust me, you will achieve success that much faster if you can find a mentor and pay attention to his or her lessons.

Greatness Lies Not in Trying to Be Somebody but Rather in Trying to Help Somebody

Financially successful people have arrived at a place and time in their lives where they are operating at peak performance. They

---

1. The Logan Hunter Group, *The Average American, Financial Casualty Report*, http://www.financialsecurity101.com/files/FIN_INDEP.pdf. 2011.

have become a productive, fine-tuned money-making machine that works on autopilot. They are no longer concerned with their status in life, as they know where they stand. They have already overcome their destructive negative ego and are more focused on a constructive ego. They have no desire to look down on anyone. Instead, they are focused on helping people who help themselves. If you want to become financially successful like them, you will need to earn their trust and worthiness of their time and mentorship. The majority of mentors have a power of discernment: they know who is genuine and who is not, and if by chance they were wrong, they will be quick to end the relationship.

If you ask a true mentor, "What is the first step in learning, in finding the fastest, most productive way of doing something and the truth of how things work?" he or she will usually answer, "The first step is to talk less, listen more, and stay humble." If you ask, "What is the second step?" the mentor would say, "Talk less, listen more, and stay humble." If you ask, "What is the third step?" he or she would say, "Talk less, listen more, and stay humble."

A mentor's hindsight can become your foresight.

Mentors have learned how to think accurately from their past experiences of trial and error. They are clear on how to separate facts from mere information. They have learned which facts are important and which are unimportant for continued success. They are a brain to pick, an ear to bend, and people who can push you in the right direction. A mentor's hindsight can work greatly to your advantage and become your foresight.

A Mentor Will Take You Where You Need to Go

Until a person figures out his definite purpose and begins to focus on whatever formula is necessary for success with his dream, he scatters his energy and thoughts in all different directions. That indecisiveness leads to weakness and lack of personal power to take action in any direction. A scattered brain creates a scattered life. A mentor helps you stay laser-light focused in the direction you need to be going.

One reason many of us never achieve what we truly want is that we never are clear about where we are going, and we don't know how to direct our focus. We don't know how to concentrate on the focus that gives us the power to achieve our dream. Most people just saunter their way through life never deciding to become great, or even good, at anything, let alone having the courage to master something.

Mentors have a keen understanding about life. The majority of them look at themselves as just ordinary people who stuck to it longer than the other guy. They know that most people have no idea of the incredible capacity inside them to focus and immediately command success by using all their internal resources so they can master something in their lives.

Focusing on a goal and chasing it is like finding a distant star that many times you feel can't be reached. However, the moment you create a plan and definitely commit yourself, believing in your goal with passion, you must focus on arriving at that distant star with conviction. As you travel closer and closer to that distant star that you never thought possible to reach, the gravity of the star eventually takes over and pulls you in, forcing you to arrive. Mentors have already experienced that forced arrival and are now focused on helping others.

Mentors Know How to Turn Others into Potential Future Mentors

Mentors have been there and done that. They know what works and what doesn't. They understand that the human person can only do what it knows to do, though it very seldom does what it does not know what to do. They know that small adjustments or decisions can net big results. True mentors will not allow you to dig holes with a shovel; rather they will introduce you to a backhoe. They have already done their research and are living successfully with the results.

Good mentors don't claim to know everything; they instead constantly humble themselves to learn more from others and are therefore pro-education and fanatical about continued education. They understand how important continued education is and that we can all learn something from each other. Otherwise, if you always do what you have always done, you will always be where you have always been, and you will always have what you have always had! Consider this: if you are responsible for earning the income for your family and responsible for your family's quality way of life, don't you think you should be investing more in your personal education and in your self-improvement? Learning from a mentor helps you reach this goal. And in return, great mentors create other great mentors. Through a mentor's guidance, you will learn not only whatever skill or trade he or she is teaching you, but you will also learn how to mentor and teach.

As you continually learn how to become better and better at your dream profession, take the time to identify all the people, groups, suppliers, or organizations that you will need cooperation or assistance from to achieve your goals. For example, after years of training people with so many different personalities, Market Traders Institute (MTI) has put together the Ultimate Traders Package, containing important information about becoming a Forex trader, accompanied by all the suppliers and organizations needed to achieve your goals.

A Mentor's Spirit to Serve

Think of the most successful people you know. What really makes them different than you? Do they have two arms and two legs? Do they have two eyes and a mouth? Do they need to eat when they get hungry and sleep when they get tired, just like you do? Of course they do. What then is the difference between you and them? After all, successful people are human beings with human emotions and human problems. There are many things that can make a person successful; however, I have found that their knowledge, their skills, and their disciplines set them apart from everyone else. It is their talent of repetitive patterns of thought, feeling, and actions. Successful people have repetitive patterns of positive thought, followed by positive feelings, followed by positive constructive actions. They have paid the price, they know how hard it is to find success, and they know it takes 10 times the amount of work to continue to stay successful after they found success. They know success is not a destination. It is a continuous journey, and the target is always moving.

Most mentors have a compassionate heart and a spirit to serve, and *they understand how hard life's battles can be.* Just about every successful person who is willing to become someone's mentor knows the price that needs to be paid for their success. Mentors know that *what they have done for themselves will die with them, but what they have done, and will do, for others in this world will become immortal.* Their help and guidance provide others a way to face their struggles.

Most people experience immortality through their children. However, a mentor experiences his immortality through helping others, teaching them a new skill, or providing them with guidance. People forget what you have said and may even forget what you did for them, but they never forget how it feels to be taught a new skill that they will be able to use the rest of their lives.

A mentor experiences his immortality
through helping others.

In my book, *The 10 Essentials of Forex Trading,* I teach the technical skills of how to trade in the Forex market. The skills I teach in that book are natural skills and methodologies that have to do with Mother Nature. They will outlive me and my posterity. With our trading courses being approved by the major universities of the world, I have learned that I can attain immortality through my courses and writings that will continue to teach others long after I have physically stopped moving. Mentors know their immortality lies not in the things they leave behind, but in the people whose lives they have touched. The skills they have taught that can change or enhance one's life forever. Perhaps even their children's lives. You can never help too much!

We all make a living by what we get, *but we all make a life by what we give.* No one knows this better than a mentor. There is a miracle in giving and receiving, and it is a quite simple age-old adage: the more we give, the more we get. One thing I keep learning is that the secret of being happy is doing things for other people. Mentors are clear that perhaps they started out focused on themselves and perhaps on their needs or the needs of the family. However, they are now past that. They have entered the realm of giving back and of showing the world their gratitude for all their opportunities and everything that has been given to them.

Learn from Your Mentor's Mistakes

Mentors have already overcome the problems that you'll encounter. They have already made the mistakes you are about to make, and they are skilled in not repeating them. In the field of trading, I have made just about every mistake possible. I have already gone through the school of hard knocks, and I have found the habits and disciplines necessary to become successful in my Forex trading endeavors. There is no need for you to bang your head against the wall for years through trial and error trying to figure out what works and what doesn't if you instead can tap into your mentor's experience and knowledge. The mentor-mentee relationship is meant to teach you how to not waste your time and not make errors that produce no income (or a serious loss of income).

A mentor knows that when we make a mistake, we learn a tremendous amount of great, life-altering information that can put our lives back on track. Wisdom is acquired when a mistake is made. A mentor will tell you that when you make a mistake, don't look back in a negative way—look back in a positive way. Don't dwell on your spilled milk. No one benefits from spilled milk, except the cat. The past cannot be changed. The here and now along with the future are what we have to deal with.

Wisdom is acquired when a mistake is made.

Mentors are those strong people who have the tenacity and courage to never give up when they make a mistake. They know that strong people make as many mistakes as weak people. The difference is that strong people admit their mistakes, laugh at them, learn from them, create ways to prevent them from happening again, and move on. That is how they become strong. Mentors who have been successful for a certain period of time in any field already have proven they cannot be intimidated by challenges, mistakes, dead ends, or brick walls. They already know that every great achievement comes with setbacks, and they have worked through those setbacks. They already know how to admit to and laugh at their own mistakes. They know that when you choose a behavior, you choose a consequence. After all, we are all nothing more than the choices we make. They are what they are today because of the decisions and mistakes they made yesterday, and that is what keeps them humble.

Any mentor will tell you that making mistakes is part of being human. They would ask how without making a mistake would you know what needs to be worked on or improved in your life? Mentors know great new disciplines are born from mistakes and that just about all of life's important lessons can only be gained from making a mistake. The only real mistake in life is the one from which we learn nothing.

Building Experience Through Our Own Mistakes

Inevitably, although you will learn a great deal through your mentor's mistakes, you too are bound to make some. Do not fear: if you pay attention while making a mistake, you will acquire experience, and experience is the name we give to our mistakes. Experience is that incredible thing inside us that allows us to recognize when another mistake is about to happen, and it helps us avoid future mistakes. Mentors realize mistakes are merely steps up the ladder of success. Every mistake that they made and took the time to learn from got them that much closer to their goal. So don't be surprised when your mentor thinks it is OK for you to mess up—your mentor may even encourage it, as long as you learn from your errors. Also, if you think you will be able to trade in the Forex without making a mistake, then you will be greatly disappointed.

I have learned that most people beat themselves up emotionally when they make a mistake, but *all traders make big mistakes*. For example, I remember a point in time in 1998 (which I discuss fully in Chapter 15). I had for years been trading and working diligently on a daily basis being disciplined in my trading strategies and habits. I was fully confident in my trading abilities—so confident that I repeated a mistake from my past and entered into a false sense of security, thinking I was above the laws of trading. I thought I could control the market, rather than the market controlling me.

Now there I was, the great and masterful FXCHIEF at his best. However, within five hours after I entered my trade, I entered that awful zone where my arrogance took hold and I found myself in the dark dungeon named "False Sense of Security." Then . . . BOOM! An atomic bomb hit my trading career. Within five hours my trading account was liquidated: $400,000—gone forever.

Learn from all your mistakes, but find a mentor, pay attention to his life lessons, and try to avoid major ones yourself. Some mistakes can be of a serious nature or life altering, have a profound impact on our lives, and change the course of our destiny. If sorrow is involved, sorrow will become your teacher. But mentors know that unless the mistake is fatal, something can always be learned to our benefit.

The true art of living is learning how to put our mistakes into perspective. One of my challenges was to pay attention to that life-altering mistake and earn all the money back more intelligently. Mentors know that making mistakes is simply the opportunity to begin the process again more intelligently. It is imperative to learn from our mistakes. If you have made mistakes, even serious ones, there is a second chance. Thank goodness that this life is full of second chances.

> The true art of living is learning how to put
> our mistakes into perspective.

The greatest belief we must have is that our mistakes are part of being human and that we can overcome them. Otherwise we would give up at trying to become successful at whatever it is we are trying to accomplish. You must realize that a mistake gives you a second chance to do it differently or to perfect it. When you make a mistake, you have to step back, understand what happened, and then put into place a new discipline enabling you to avoid making that mistake again. The problem will arise when you become tempted to make that same mistake again; you do not want to become a habitual offender. Mentors are not habitual offenders; they know what works and what doesn't.

Mentors know that everyone makes mistakes. However, as you work through your mistakes, mentors act as coaches, encouraging you to say, "I can get over this and move on. I can do this!" Mentors help you realize you are not alone at making mistakes. Everyone makes mistakes. What you can't do is be afraid of making a mistake when you are learning something new. Some people are so embarrassed about their mistakes they go and hide, thinking the world saw what they did. I was playing a game with my four nieces. I started to notice that my one niece would never attempt to answer a question she did not know. When I asked her why she was doing that, she said, "I hate making mistakes and being wrong. So I would rather not say or do anything, unless I know I am going to be right."

Most people think making a mistake is doing something that did not work or does not work. That is not necessarily true. What is true is that there is a big difference between making a mistake and deliberately making a conscious effort to do something wrong. When we deliberately and consciously do something wrong, that is not a mistake! When traders learn a hard-and-fast rule at trading and then deliberately disobey the rule or deliberately break that rule, that is not a mistake. That is an act of doing something they want to do.

Conclusion

If you are serious about your success, find other successful people who have already made the mistakes and learn from them to help you avoid making the same ones. Let them teach you. They already know that falling down is not the mistake, but staying down is. If you have tried to become successful at anything and were met with setbacks and defeat, you are not alone. Every great achievement is filled with setbacks and defeats. Your defeats are nothing more than installments into the other bank account named Victory.

Don't fear those defeats or failures; embrace them. If you have created hopes, dreams, and plans and watched them all crumble before your eyes, just remember that the greatest people in all of history went through the same thing. They are all ultimately products of courage and tenacity, and they understand that greatness is found in never giving up, even after making potentially life-altering mistakes. Incredible adversity along with mistakes gives birth to opportunity and patiently lies in the cradle of success. What one calls a dead end from a mistake is what another calls the birth of an opportunity.

Mentors know what works and what doesn't work. Find a person you respect and admire and who is successful in the field, and ask that person to help you—to mentor you. Get to know that person, find out what his or her habits are, and begin to emulate that person. It's not that mentors are so smart, it is just that they stuck with their problems a little longer than the average person and figured out the problems so they could become successful. They persisted long enough to figure out exactly what needed to be done. Many people have gone further than they thought they could because they had a mentor who cared, led the way, and told them they could do it.

Successful people who can become your mentor have discovered a formula that works in their expertise. Their daily focus is to be disciplined about holding to that formula. Not finding a mentor can dramatically hold you back from achieving what you want out of life.

CHAPTER 3

GREED AND FEAR CONTROL THE MARKET

Poverty and mediocrity want much, but greed wants everything. Greed has only one object and that is to wrongfully take, consume, and ultimately destroy everything it touches and is near. It has no feeling or pity for the devastating consequences or destruction it causes the people, even loved ones, you know. It is ruthlessly ready to destroy everything that is beautiful in your life without notice. It does not care who or what you are, and it is not capricious. It doesn't hesitate to crush the life out of any human being who gets in its way. It takes what it wants from anyone and anything regardless of any consequences. It moves as if it were above the law. Greed has no time limit to its ultimate destruction. When its hungry appetite surfaces and awakens inside you, it lies to your soul and promises you the world. Greed makes you believe that money, and money alone, is life's answer to all questions. It is more addictive than a drug. And like a drug, it causes you to constantly look for a new high—something more to acquire at whatever cost. It instills the belief that there is always something more to acquire at whatever cost. Do not fail to recognize it in your life. If you are currently in greed's way, *run* . . . get as far away from it as you possibly can, at any cost, or you will become its next victim!

Out of all the sayings I have taught my children, two really stand out as related to this chapter. I hope you adopt them in your life as I have in mine:

- When greed exceeds your need, it will usually take you down a path of self-destruction.
- Control your excesses.

How you deal with greed in your life will affect your habits at the trading table. I will never forget one year when opportunity knocked at the door of a friend of mine. He found an investment that sounded too good to be true with an incredible return of 400 percent a year. After pestering me over and over again to get involved, I warned him that such returns just don't last and without being able to do some clear due diligence on the company, I would rather pass and wish him well.

> How you deal with greed in your life will
> affect your habits at the trading table.

Eventually, however, after watching him receive huge dividend checks over the next two years, I just had to succumb, get involved, and invest. I planned to invest $20,000, which my friend chided me for.

"Come on," he said, "You are worth so much more! Put in at least a million. Within a year it will be worth $4 million." I said, "You might be correct, but you might be incorrect. If they stay in business and pay me, my million will turn into $4 million; if they go out of business, my million will be gone forever. I refuse to risk more than $20,000. It is an amount that will not change my life if this opportunity goes bad or I lose all of it. It will not create a financial or emotional burden or threat to my family, lifestyle, emotional happiness, or physical well-being. *You got it?*"

So I invested the $20,000. Within 60 days, I received a check for $9,000. My friend urged me to reinvest the $9,000 to yield even higher returns within the next 60 days. I told him I would rather wait another 60 days, receive another check for $9,000 to

$11,000, and get all my money back before moving forward with no risk of loss or downside on my investment. I told him, "At least I know what I got; I don't know what I will get."

As time went on, my friend believed this glittering object of an opportunity was nothing but pure gold and kept sending back the majority of the money he was making, short of buying a larger home with a larger mortgage and a fancy car with a bigger car payment. He even quit his job; he and his wife lived on the income he was making from his investment. As real estate was booming, his house increased in value, so he went out and refinanced it to take out as much equity as possible. He had put his entire hope in this one opportunity, taking all of his savings and cash and continuing to invest all he had in this one investment.

Well as the saying goes, when it sounds too good to be true, it usually is too good to be true. Sure enough, as I was waiting for my other check for $9,000 to $11,000, the state attorney's office came in and declared the activities of the company to be a Ponzi scheme and shut it down. The loss I incurred was only the balance of my $11,000, a loss I could live with. But as for my friend, he lost everything. While the state attorney's office was conducting their investigation, my friend could not eat, sleep, or even think—he was so consumed by the devastation and the collapse of his dream. He came over every day claiming that his life was over.

Failing to look at the potential downside of his investment completely altered his life. After everything was settled by the government, it was announced no one would get any more returns and that the company was bankrupt. My friend was emotionally, physically, and financially devastated. He told me on several occasions he just wanted to commit suicide because he had no money, no savings, no job, and no income. All he had were debts beyond his capability to pay. As time passed, stress took its toll and he ended up having a heart attack at the age of 46 after he lost his house, his car, his life savings, and sadly to say, even his marriage and family.

Greed, Money, and Happiness

Was it worth it? Is it ever worth it? Of course not, but when we let the seed of greed be planted in our minds and hearts, and allow it to grow wild, it changes our lives forever. The outcome is always life-altering for the worse. It whispers deception and lies, promising wealth, health, and happiness. It entices with all its charm and tempts us to keep going because enough is never enough. Well disguised, it is there like a virus multiplying in our hearts and minds, a capricious monster that is never satisfied. Greed has only one objective, and that is to seek and destroy. It ultimately consumes and destroys everything it touches and everything in its surrounding path. The unpredictability of greed means it has no printed expiration date to warn us against poisoning or fatal effects. And if greed poisons us or kills us in the end, it has no remorse and no sorrow for the calamity it brings into our lives. It claims no responsibility for the destruction it causes. It crouches in wait, ruthlessly ready to destroy what is beautiful, without notice. It does not show partiality and will crush the life out of any human being who begins to buy into the lie that money and money alone is the answer to life's happiness.

We tend to forget that happiness doesn't come as a result of buying or acquiring something we don't have, but rather from learning to appreciate what we already have. While my friend was losing everything, my emotional and financial life maintained its stability because I have learned never to risk more than I can afford to lose, always keeping in mind that not everything I might want in life is everything I need.

Happiness doesn't come as a result of buying or acquiring something we don't have, but rather from learning to appreciate what we already have.

The key is to never risk anything that will alter your existing lifestyle. It just isn't worth it in the end. Happiness, peace of mind, and life's fulfillment is managing your wants versus your needs in your life: Mother Nature provides enough to satisfy every man's need, but not every man's greed.

Our society is motivated by greed. Advertising, marketing, and commercials on TV don't make it easier for us. As a matter of fact, they instill in us those dangerous seeds of greed, telling us we will not be happy unless we buy, use, or consume what they advertise. They try to sell us incredible cars, clothes, electronics, homes, and exotic vacations that all cost money and are well beyond the average person's income!

Now a major trend is taking place in which buying, selling, and making money online through using your computer at home, or anywhere in the world, is possible. Craigslist, eBay, Backpage, and even online trading companies are participating in that new trend. Right now it is heavily being advertised that the new, untraditional wave of investing and creating phenomenal wealth is via the Internet from the comfort of your own home. Sounds great, but the question remains: how are you going to learn what you are doing?

Ninety-five percent of the world looks at trading as a fantasy get-rich-quick scheme, and they enter the market simply based on greed. If you want to become a Forex trader, it needs to be one of your well-thought-out and well-planned dreams, not just some type of moneymaking ploy. If the stresses from all the complications from debts in your life are driving you to get involved in trading—thinking that making fast money from the market might be the answer to resolving your financial stresses—you better think again. Learning to trade is a disciplined profession.

After beginning a trading career and facing a couple weeks of limited progress by breaking even or incurring outright losses, many new traders are quick to rethink their involvement in the market. Any loss of money becomes painful as you look back and scary as you look forward.

When Greed Creates Fear

When a trader starts taking losses or enters into an area of vulnerability, fear sets in and trading is no longer fun and games. Because of greed, many people are brought to the trading table with the thought of fast money and the potential for easy living, after all . . . he who is greedy is always in want.

The greatest barrier to most successes is the fear of failure. What is your greatest fear in your life right now? What is your greatest fear in trading? When I was learning, my greatest fear was of running out of money before I learned a successful trading methodology so I could consistently make money.

> The greatest barrier to success is the fear of failure.

A human's deepest fear is not of being inadequate, but of knowing in its heart that it is capable of becoming successful and powerful beyond measure once it conquers its fear of responsibility. It is that light of potential, not the darkness of failure, that frightens us. Being responsible for our actions creates fear. People fear success because they then need to be responsible for their actions. Most unsuccessful people prefer being unsuccessful. As long as they are struggling, they have an excuse to blame their lack of success on some other person or thing. The moment they become successful, they are responsible for their destiny and that scares everyone to death.

Fear forces us to challenge ourselves by saying, "Who am I to think that I am smart enough, talented enough, outright fabulous enough, or skillful enough to accomplish this task?" From experience, there are times you must rise to the occasion, defy all your past destructive beliefs and demons that hold you back, and say, "Nothing good can happen in my life if I start shrinking away from my potential. We are all meant to shine and reach our highest potential in whatever field we choose in our life, even if that field is trading." Pretending to be a nobody or just another person in this world doesn't serve you or the world. You must figure out your purpose.

It is in all of us, every one of us, to shine and reach our highest potential. As we develop the courage to attack our fears, we subconsciously give ourselves permission to start to achieve great things. We liberate ourselves from our own fears, and the courage we have to confront those fears begins to open the doors of success. Each time we face our fears, we gain strength, courage, and confidence in what we are attempting to accomplish.

Living and Trading with Fear

There are only two ways to live your life:

- In a state of fear, you maintain a feeling that everything you are learning or doing in life is not going to work out to your long-term benefit. Fearing that you just can't do this or that, you make excuses every day about your life as to why you cannot achieve greatness.
- Believing nothing is impossible, you have a strong daily hope that you will figure it out. If it were not for having hope that you could figure things out, your heart would break. Without hope, people perish. You wouldn't know what to do next in life if it weren't for hope of achievement.

Learning to trade needs to be about merging your thought processes and emotions with the movement of the market—not with fear, but only with constant hope that you can and will derive an income or return on your investment of time that you are spending at trading. Blindly hoping for success, however, will not lead to success. Too much hope as a beginner trader will place you in a position of being too creative and overconfident. It can work against you. The saddest thing I have seen is overconfident traders who are quickly introduced to failure by not addressing the downside of trading and protecting themselves as they trade. That ignorance or lack of discipline creates fear the next time they trade. I have watched them as their dreams start washing down the financial drain due to stupid undisciplined decisions and mistakes, causing their money to slowly run out before they learn how to trade effectively.

Markets are driven by greed and fear. We get into the markets out of greed and get out due to fear. As fear is based on something that we think may happen in the future, it is clearly a mental process that tries to predict the future—in that sense, the reason for the fear is a projection of our mind. We can be afraid to fall, but once we are falling, we are afraid to hit the ground. Once we hit the ground, we may fear we are badly injured. Once we know we are badly injured, we may fear the pain and consequences of not being able to work for some time or becoming disabled. So one could say that fear is always based on something that has not happened yet and is therefore a fantasy of our mind rather than fact. In trading, fear has a large shadow, but it is really a small object to overcome and conquer. In life, as well as in trading, there are four ways to handle fear: you can go over it, you can go under it, you can even go around it, but to put fear behind you, enabling you to conquer your dream, you must walk straight through it.

Many traders are afraid to show the world who they really are. They fear that if they expose themselves the world may not accept them or like them, because that is all they have to offer. Inadequacy breeds doubts and fears. Learning a skill like trading can change that. It can breed confidence and courage. If you want to conquer your fear, do not simply sit and think about it; write down the things you fear the most and then put a plan in place of how you are going to tackle each of them. Go out and make it happen. By overcoming your fears, you change your outlook on life and even the outcome of your life. Don't fear stepping outside of your comfort zone. Do the thing you fear the most and keep on doing it; that is the best way to prove to yourself that you have conquered your fear!

In trading, there are two kinds of fear. One kind is the fear that prevents you from taking action. For example, if you are long without a stop and the market is falling like a rock, you need to take action and get out now! Another kind of fear is one of respect.

You must approach the market with a healthy fear and the utmost respect. To the unprepared, it can and will take all your money and drown you financially without any hesitation or guilt.

You can't truly fear what you haven't experienced. Your negative experience is the birth of the fear in your soul. You block your dream of becoming whatever you are trying to achieve when you allow your fear to grow bigger than the faith or hope that you can accomplish what you have set out to do.

We get involved in trading because of excitement. We see a way to make money on our terms: staying at home; not having a boss, employees, inventory or receivables, or headaches; and making money 24 hours a day at our convenience. Then whack, your greed gets the best of you and you take your first loss—the money has gone right out of your account.

You say, "No problem, they told me about this." Then whack, another loss and more money is gone. Now you're a little concerned. Then comes another whack, another surprise, and even more money is gone. You are now taken aback and concerned.

Unlike losses in our daily lives, market losses are quick and nonnegotiable. The money you lose is automatically taken out of your account. You have no say. The only things you have say over while trading are your decisions of entries and exits. When you lose in a trade, you see all this money gone and you are now scared and fearful. Your judgment is challenged. Your ego is challenged. Your self-esteem is challenged. Your common sense is challenged. More important, everyone you told about this is watching you and expecting a favorable report.

Embrace the Market with Caution

The next time you pull the trigger to trade, quantify your potential loss and then ask yourself, "Can I afford to take the loss should the trade not work out? Yes or no?" If the answer is no, don't pull the trigger; it is that simple. Don't get sucked in by your greed. Know your boundaries!

If the answer is yes, enter the trade and move forward hoping for the best and preparing for the worst. If you have set up the trade wisely, the worst thing that can happen is your quantified stop-loss order is hit and you lose a determined amount of money that you already decided you could live with losing.

If you are an active trader who is dealing with the fear of losing money, what are you going to do about it? Finding a simple productive trading strategy with a set of rules that you will be disciplined enough to obey will place you in a position of conquering your fear, providing you with the necessary confidence that will allow you to stop losing more money than you make. Either you control your fear, or your fear controls you!

Either you control your fear, or your fear controls you!

The only way you can get back on track is to believe you can overcome your fear with courage while maintaining a positive attitude. Muster up all the courage you can find and move forward saying: "I don't fear the market. I embrace it! I do have a fearful and healthy respect for it, so I refuse to succumb to any fear or greed. Losses are a part of this game, and I am going to turn my trading scars into trading stars. Nothing in this life or in this market is going to scare me. If it does, I am going to have the courage to address my fear and plow through it. This market or my life is not to be feared. It is only to be understood, and I can understand everything about it, because I believe I am an intelligent human being. I came into this life and trading to succeed, not to be paralyzed by fear or tempted by greed but to conquer fear and greed and overcome failure."

You will not become a good trader if you are plagued with fear. Fear is a mind killer. It is the little death that brings total obliteration and destruction to your trading. Fear is that darkroom where all your negatives are created. Ultimately, you know that to develop into a successful trader, you will have to bring those negatives out of the darkroom and into the light to be exposed. You have to face your fear head-on with all the courage in the world, or it will start to control you and it won't go away. You gain strength, courage, and confidence in every situation where you stop to look fear in the face. You must do the thing that you think you cannot do.

Security in the market is a superstition: it does not exist. When you get a little experience coupled with success under your belt, be careful because you can easily step into an arena of false security. That is why people drown in the ocean. They swim with insufficient respect for the ocean and a false sense of security that they are greater than the force of the ocean. What is amazing is the ocean meant no harm. It was just doing what it does on a daily basis. Like the ocean, the market exists with no feeling. So without a proper respect and fear for the market, you too can drown financially. Trust me, the market will have no mercy! Why? It can't feel and it can't care. The only way you avoid danger in the market is to properly understand what the market is capable of doing to you.

Hope and Fear in the Market

Most traders are confused about how to use the terms *hope* and *fear* in the market and apply them backward. When the market is racing in the opposite direction, most traders immediately begin hoping it will come back. They hope and pray, then pray and hope, and then hope and pray some more, when in fact they should be fearing their losses, not hoping they come back. Now if in fact the market does come back, they are quick to get out with a small profit because they fear the market will take away whatever profits they make.

I have seen traders enter into trades, watch the market move three weeks in the opposite direction going 2,000 pips against them, and pray and hope for those three weeks that it will come back. If the market does come back after they live in pain with sleepless nights for three weeks, they get out with 10 pips in profit due to the fear the market will take it back way from them. Wow! They risk 2,000 pips to capture 10. Not a good formula for trading success.

You see, they have their fear and hope mixed up and need to reverse their application in the market. They should be fearful of losses and quick to get out with a small loss if the market starts to move against them. Fearing your losses means protecting yourself at all times and trading with tight protective stop-loss orders. If a trade starts to go their way and run in their direction, they need to let it run, hoping it will keep running. A successful trader needs to fear his losses and hope that his profits run.

Hoping your profits run means understanding where the market is going in a larger time frame and then entering on a smaller time frame, quantifying your losses on the smaller time frame and then projecting your profits on a larger time frame. Let it run! Don't fear that the market gets to your target—*hope* it gets to your target.

You must have hope in every trade. Without it, trading would be miserable. True hope dwells on the possible, even when you feel trading seems to be a plot written by the market, which you believe wants to see how much misery and adversity it can give you just to see if you can overcome it. While the market fluctuates during our trades, we go through the emotions of fear, excitement, hope, and greed. Once the market returns back to break even, or even rallies 5 or 10 pips in our favor after we go through such hell, we once again fear that the market is going to take those 5 or 10 pips away. However, we must fear our losses and let our profits run. When the market gets back to our break-even, we need to let it continue to move in our direction with hope, not fear.

Here are some questions to ponder, pause and reflect:

- When you trade, are you more fearful or hopeful?
- Do you enter trades feeling more fearful or more hopeful?
- Do you consider yourself to be more optimistic or more pessimistic? If you consider the world a cup, is yours usually half empty or half full?

If you are pessimistic, there is a high probability you will be filled with fear and thoughts of failure when trading. You will trade with the mindset of expecting the worst and will have a high probability of subconsciously setting yourself up for failure. When you are in fear of failure and constantly think about failure, failure usually becomes the end result, as what we think about usually happens. More important, because you are so consumed with the thoughts of failure, you will subconsciously miss a detail that will blindside you and hurt you financially.

The opposite takes place if you are optimistic, are filled with hope, and avoid thoughts of greed. You will have a high probability of succeeding in your trades. When you learn the emotional skills involved in trading, you will allow yourself to be calm, maintaining your sense of logic and emotional intelligence from your training.

Hope sees the invisible, feels the possibilities, touches the realities, and achieves the impossible. With hope you can clearly see your future success while blurring your past failures. Hope sees the sunshine, while fear and failure see the storms.

> Hope sees the invisible, feels the possibilities, touches the realities, and achieves the impossible.

Hope is not the conviction that something will turn out well, but the certainty that something (the formula) makes sense regardless of how it turns out. There are no hopeless situations in trading, only hopeless traders who allow their belief systems to go bad. Trading is a lot like football. You have to tackle your problems, block your fears, and score your points when you get the opportunity.

Conclusion

Humans are complex beings, and their habit is not to keep things simple. They believe value is added if they can complicate the process, whether through their systems or emotions. They feel they are gaining value when they are creative, making new rules or taking greedy risks, going against their training. Some traders want to add more bells and whistles to their systems instead of following what they've been taught. More rules make them feel important. In reality, they are going in the wrong direction.

Don't reinvent this wheel. Don't waste your trading experience creating new systems and strategies. They have already been created by some of the best traders in the world. No need to give birth to doubts and fears from your own creations. Spend your time educating yourself both technically and emotionally, so you can deal with the roller-coaster of greed, fear, and hope in the market. Spend your time figuring out a simple strategy that constantly works. If you want success, keep it simple, avoid greed, confront your fears, and hope for the best. When you become good at a strategy and when you learn to trade with confidence, it is then that you should not be afraid to go out on a limb, because after all, that's where the fruit is.

CHAPTER 4

ACHIEVING EXCELLENCE AT TRADING

Aristotle stated, "Excellence is an art won by training and habitu- ation. We do not act rightly because we have virtue or excel- lence, but we rather have those because we have acted rightly. We are what we repeatedly do. Excellence, then, is not an act or a one- time event, it is a habit."

A life of excellence is not just a skill; it is a decision. Excellence is rare. Instead, worry, envy, jealousy, hatred, doubt, and fear are com- mon and fatal to achieving excellence. True winners do not become winners when they win an event or achieve something great. They become winners because of their dedication to excellence in the hours, days, weeks, and years they spent preparing for their suc- cess. Their successful performance is merely a demonstration of their commitment to excellence and their true character of being a champion.

If you think bad things are not going to happen to you in your life, then you are grossly mistaken. If you think bad things are not going to happen as you learn to trade, then you better never even entertain the idea of becoming a trader. How you handle adversity in your life will determine the quality of life you will or will not be able to enjoy. How you handle mishaps as you trade will determine whether or not you make it as a successful trader.

In times of severe financial crises or wrongdoing, your true char- acter is not developed; rather, it is revealed, and your reputation is either built or destroyed. It is a sad day when people let money or the loss of money dictate their actions and negotiate their character. The weak are always forced to decide between alternatives they themselves have not chosen. Weakness of attitude becomes weakness of character. Some people aren't used to a life or an environment of excellence. The lessons of the ordinary are everywhere. Original and profound insights are only found by studying the exemplary.

> A life of excellence is not just a skill, it is a decision.

I have always struggled with figuring things out at trading. It has taken me longer than the average person. My persistence at trading, however, has taught me that if you achieve anything without a struggle, it probably was not worth achieving. One of the greatest discoveries people make in life, one of their great surprises, occurs when hanging on to a goal after others let go. While working through those darkest hours, people find they can do what they were afraid at first they couldn't do. That is what sets these people apart from others: that tenacity to not let go as so many others do. Like uncut diamonds, many individuals have shining capabilities beneath a rough, unpolished exterior, and they need help in uncovering or unveiling them.

I hope I am one of those people who can help you discover those great traits that are hidden perhaps deep inside you but very able to come out. Many great things in life are only achieved because people took the time to educate themselves on how to achieve them and then had the courage to pursue them. What we learn in life with a desire to do it right or have it be well done is well done forever!

So what are you here to do as you live your life on earth? What are you here trying to achieve as you read this book?

Before you continue to read this chapter, answer the following:

- What are you here to accomplish as a trader?
- Are you here looking for some sort of financial return with limited emotional satisfaction?

- Are you truly here to learn the skills, techniques, attitudes, and disciplines of a great trader? Are you here to learn the emotional and psychological makeup of a great trader, or are you here to just achieve some sort of an emotional high?
- Are you here to satisfy some sort of egotistical need in your life?
- Are you here trying to turn trading into a part-time hobby?
- Are you really aware that mental success comes before the actual physical success?
- Are you here to become that perfect trader that everyone reads about?

No matter how you answer the preceding questions, you need to understand that perfection at trading, or anything in life, cannot actually be achieved, because it does not exist. However, perfection can be pursued with diligence, and in doing so it is possible to reach excellence.

One of the most essential things you need to do for yourself as you learn to trade is to choose a goal that is important to you, realizing that perfection at that goal does not exist, but excellence at that goal does. As you work to achieve that goal, realize you can always do better. When human beings strive to do better, they can be sure about always growing and moving in the right direction.

Perfection Does Not Exist, but Excellence Does

Excellence at trading not only needs to be learned, but it needs to become a habit, remember Aristotle's words. You cannot be good at trading just every now and then and succeed; you need to be consistently great at trading to survive in the market. Keep in mind, we are not looking for home runs; we are looking to get to first base over and over: consistency is key.

Farmers can make mistakes as they plant their crops, but the crops don't lie—when they come up, they show the line, however straight or crooked. Regardless of how you feel about trading, your account statement proves to you and the world your ability or inability to trade.

When we aim for excellence, we soon learn it is a moving target. We must be willing to move and adapt as the target of excellence moves. We cannot live in self-denial, thinking our definition of excellence is the only one that exists. Everyone has a very different perception of the term *excellence*. To some traders making 100 pips a month is excellent; to others the mark of excellence is 400 pips.

When we aim for excellence, we soon learn it is a moving target.

If you were asked to share your definition of excellence at trading, what would it be? I would think that everyone might have a little variation but would end up agreeing that excellence in trading would most definitely mean making a consistent profit at trading.

We most certainly all have dreams when it comes time to execute our trades. But making dreams become a reality requires a great deal of determination, dedication, self-discipline, and effort. People can be as great as they want to be. If they believe in themselves and have these qualities along with courage, a competitive drive, and a willingness to sacrifice who they are for who they need to become, they have a chance at becoming excellent. You must learn to sacrifice in your life to succeed at what you believe is worthwhile. Never forget: human beings can achieve anything they want to achieve. If you are going to achieve excellence in the big things in life, you have to first make it a habit of achieving excellence in the little things in life. I am eternally grateful to my mom and dad for making me resweep the floors as a child over and over until I got it right. I am grateful for the many hours they made me reclean the family bathroom or revacuum—the list goes on. Like all kids, at the time I thought they were just punishing me, but the reality is they were teaching me habits of being excellent in small things so when I grew up I could become excellent in larger ways.

Excellence is an attitude and the gradual result of always wanting to do or be better at whatever you are attempting. Carpenters and craftsmen both possess the same tools. Carpenters use theirs to build a house; craftsmen use theirs to build castles. The same tools are used to build each structure, yet the talent and vision are very different. Having the attitude and characteristic of excellence in your life means having the unlimited ability to improve the quality of life for those around you and enhance what you have to offer. Excellence cannot be the exception; it has to be the prevailing rule, habit, and attitude in your life. If it is not, you will struggle in becoming a successful trader.

Balance Leads to Excellence

The following story was shared with me from Trisha Colloto, one of our students from Sydney, Australia:

A professor stood before his philosophy class with some items in front of him. When the class began, he wordlessly picked up a very large and empty mayonnaise jar and proceeded to fill it with golf balls. He then asked the students if the jar was full. They agreed that it was.

The professor then picked up a box of pebbles and poured them into the jar. He shook the jar gently. The pebbles fell down and settled into the open spaces between the golf balls. He then asked the students again if the jar was full. They agreed that it was.

The professor next picked up a box of sand and poured it into the jar. Of course, the sand settled and worked its way into all the cracks, filling up everything else. He asked once more if the jar was full. The students responded with a unanimous yes.

The professor then produced two cups of coffee from under the table and poured the entire contents into the jar, effectively filling the empty space between the sand. The students laughed.

"Now," said the professor as the laughter subsided, "I want you to recognize that this jar represents your life. The golf balls are the important things—your family, your children, your health, your friends, and your favorite passions—and if everything else was lost and only they remained, your life would still be full. The pebbles are the other things that matter, like your job, your house, and your car. The sand is everything else—the small stuff.

> When our lives are in balance, the results from our efforts in anything we do gravitate toward excellence.

"If you put the sand into the jar first," he continued, "there is no room for the pebbles or the golf balls. The same goes for life. If you spend all your time and energy on the small stuff, you will never have room for the things that are important to you.

"Pay attention to the things that are critical and that bring you happiness. Play with your children. Take time to get medical checkups. Take your spouse out to dinner. Play another 18 holes. There will always be time to clean the house and fix the disposal. Take care of the golf balls first—the things that really matter. Set your priorities. The rest is just sand."

One of the students raised her hand and inquired what does the coffee represent? The professor smiled, "I'm glad you asked." It just goes to show you that no matter how full your life may seem, there's always room for a couple cups of coffee with a friend."

A quality life is never an accident; it is always the result of putting your life into perspective with high intention, sincere effort, intelligent direction, and skillful execution. A quality life reflects the wise choices we make in our daily lives out of the many alternatives we have. When our lives are in balance, the results from our efforts in anything we do gravitate toward excellence. Making a commitment to excellence in your life is not what others expect of you, it is what you give others.

You need to realize there's much more to your life than your job or your possessions. If you create a true work-life balance, you will find greater success in all facets of your life, professionally and personally. In doing so, your ability to trade with a clear mind and a successful attitude will result in greater performance.

Embracing Change to Continually Do Better

The famous football coach Vince Lombardi said: "The quality of a person's life is in direct proportion to their commitment to excellence, regardless of their chosen field of endeavor." Excellence is the gradual result of always striving to do better at whatever we do: it is found in willingness to change and in paying attention to the details as we evolve and transform.

Many of us love predictability and consistency and hate change. We want the results that come from change, but many times we do not want to change to get the results. Change frustrates the majority of mankind; however, progress cannot be made without change.

Change is the end result of all true learning. Change involves three key components:

- A personal dissatisfaction with one's self—a felt void or feeling of a need to become better, to achieve more, to want more, or to have more
- A conscious decision to do and change whatever it takes to fill the void, that need, that missing piece in your life
- A conscious dedication to the process needed for growth and change—the conscious daily willful act of making the change, consciously doing something every day that takes you closer to your goal or desired end result

To begin any change in your life, you need that goal or that beacon to look toward and then you need to hold yourself responsible for all actions that result from your focused goal. You need to create a higher standard for yourself, one that is greater than any standard that anyone expects of you, never making excuses for yourself.

Change is the end result of all true learning.

The traits and ideals that are your goals need to be like stars you cannot immediately touch but can move toward. Like any distant star, you will not immediately succeed in touching it with your hand, but like the sea-fearing man out on the ocean, you choose it as your guide, following it until you reach your destiny.

Eight Elements of Excellence

Here are "eight elements of excellence" that can guide you from the dream of excellence to the actual end result of daily applied excellence.

1. **Work with purpose and with passion.** Know why you're doing what you're doing. If you're not sure, ask. Don't be afraid to challenge anything you are being told or taught. If you have a better idea, work through your idea to see if it is better. Don't assume anything. Brainstorm all ideas, and do not shoot them down. Consider a variety of ideas, and choose the best one that works for you. You are uniquely different; never feel embarrassed about this—embrace it. As you learn to trade, what you learn needs to fit in with your personality. Once you have answered the questions of how all this information is applicable in your daily trading life and you put it into perspective, then go after it with all the excitement and energy in the world. Excellence is when you do a common thing in an uncommon way.

2. **First identify questions, and then find answers.** Learning a new skill like learning to trade involves answering your personal and unique questions that enable you to apply the new-

found knowledge in your life. Work from questions, not from conclusions. When we ask questions, we usually pay attention to the answers. It is the clear answers that help us understand where we are going. Be open to finding answers that will surprise you. Any thought that is passed on to the subconscious often and convincingly enough is eventually accepted.

3. **Be clear about your purpose.** "A man without a purpose is like a ship without a rudder," as Stephen Covey says. Begin with the end in mind. Why are you doing what you are doing, and what is it you are trying to achieve? You are not here to make money; you are here to learn the art of capturing pips. Don't confuse the two. Genius is the gold in the mine; talent is the miner who works and can understand how to properly extract the gold from the mine without killing himself out of greed or stupidity.

4. **Venture from your comfort zone.** Don't just think outside the box, act outside the box. Most of our obstacles would melt away if, instead of cowering before them, we should make up our minds to walk boldly through them. Practice paves the way to find those obstacles that need to be overcome. Obstacles are those frightful things you see when you take your eyes off your goal. Do not try to dance better than anyone else; only try to dance better than yourself. Make the most of yourself, for that is the most you can do.

5. **Strive for perfection, but aim for excellence.** Strive for perfection in everything you do, though in most things it is unattainable. As you aim for perfection and persevere, you will achieve excellence and will come much nearer to it than those whose laziness and despondency make them give it up as unattainable. As you strive for perfection, aim for excellence, not perfection. The freedom to be your best means nothing unless you are willing to do your best. The difference between the impossible and the possible lies in determination. Whatever you do, don't do it halfway. Well done is better than well said. Paint a masterpiece daily. Always autograph your work with excellence.

6. **Take risks, and never give up your right to be wrong.** Then you will lose the ability to learn new things and move forward with your life. Challenge everything, even authority. It is better to do something imperfectly than to do nothing flawlessly. Good, better, best: never let it rest till your good is better and your better is best.

7. **Respect yourself and each other.** People are intelligent and should never be treated as if they are ignorant. The way we work and act should show we respect all things and mankind. The quality of our work and our conduct should show we respect ourselves. Central to that respect is commitment to accuracy, ethics, and integrity. The foundation of lasting self-confidence and self-esteem is excellence, mastery of your work.

8. **Search for excellence as you strive to keep perfection in perspective.** Be careful not to confuse excellence with perfection. Excellence we can reach for; perfection is God's business. Every day push yourself. Excellence consists not in doing extraordinary things, but in doing ordinary things extraordinarily well. Striving for excellence motivates you; striving for perfection is demoralizing. The pursuit of perfection often impedes improvement. Artists who seek perfection in everything are those who cannot attain it in anything. All things excellent are as difficult as they are rare.

Tiger Woods said, "I just try to be the best I can be and hope that is the best ever. I give attention to the details and it seems excellence follows." Where there is life, there is hope. Where there are hopes, there are dreams. Where vivid dreams are repeated, there are goals. Goals become the action plans and game plans that winners dwell on in intricate detail, knowing that achievement is almost automatic when the goal becomes an inner commitment to excellence. The response to the challenges of life and its purpose is a commitment to excellence. A commitment to a life of excellence is the healing balm that enables each of us to face up to adversity and strife.

The response to the challenges of life and its
purpose is a commitment to excellence.

Conclusion

For some traders, learning to trade on the Forex is so overwhelming it is like learning how to build a car from scratch without an instruction manual. Many of you have acquired good parts, like brakes, wheels, motors, seats, steering wheels, and so on. Yet as you have attempted to put them together, you are still scratching your head wondering why all those parts are not creating that perfect little car you thought you could make.

Some may have an instruction manual that doesn't make sense, or, they have a proper instruction manual but are missing parts. Either way, to become successful traders you need the right parts with the right manual, enabling you to put all these parts together to make your car work properly. After all, it can take only a simple inexpensive part like a two-dollar gasket to bring your car to a screeching halt.

People trade according to their personalities. People who go through life with an attitude of poverty or mediocrity very seldom find the success they are looking for. They seem to lack a dedication to excellence, and they do not have a person in their life who forces them to resweep the floor or reclean the bathroom.

People may forget how fast you did a job, but they never forget how well you did it. As you strive to become an excellent trader, always do your best. Something magical takes place when people dedicate their lives to excellence. Their relationships are enriched, their job production and performance improve, their happiness transforms them, and, most important, their achievements escalate as they begin to live their life of success.

CHAPTER 5

UNDERSTANDING HOW YOUR HEAD AND HEART WORK

The brain gives the heart its insight. The heart gives the brain its vision. Just about everyone is somewhat intelligent. Nonetheless, there are times in life when smart people act unintelligently. You may ask, how could someone of such obvious intelligence do something so downright dumb, so illogical, and so irrational? The answer is that intellectual intelligence has very little to do with emotional intelligence.

Intellectually intelligent traders with high IQs many times have extreme difficulty governing their emotions when they trade. Traders are of course human, and though they think with their head, many times they trade with their heart, leading to self-destruction.

The next question is if traders are so smart, how is it they do not know how to control their emotions or actions? Everyone's actions come from thought first, usually accompanied with some sort of emotion. A part of everyone's actions comes from the subconscious mind, and a part comes from their subconscious belief system.

First we have the head that thinks, and then we have the heart that feels. A large part of life is learning how to manage the relationship between the two. It is like trying to distinguish between our needs and wants in our lives. We need a car to get from point A to point B. However, many people want more than just a car to get them from A to B; they want a car that feeds their ego, even at the cost of incarcerating themselves financially.

How Our Minds Work

We have three segments of the mind: one that thinks, one that feels, and one that creates an action and ultimately determines our habits. The three distinct portions or areas of the mind interact to help us conduct our mental and emotional lives:

- The rational or conscious mind (left brain)
- The powerful, impulsive, and often illogical or emotional-feeling mind (right brain)
- The subconscious mind that creates an action from our conscious logical thought or perhaps our illogical emotional feelings and creates subconscious actions that turn into subconscious habits

As we attempt to govern our lives with both our head and heart, trying to manage our wants versus our needs, we need to understand how the brain works and the critical part it plays in communicating with our heart. The brain is divided into the left brain and right brain. The left brain is considered the "head" or thinking brain from where we derive all of our logic. The right side of the brain is considered the "heart" or the feeling side of the brain from where we derive all of our feelings and emotions. In other words as the saying goes: "Our head thinks and our heart feels."

But that is not exactly true, because all that thinking and feeling is really coming out of our brain, which is placed in our head, not in our heart. Even though the world refers to feelings of the heart, it is really feelings of the head, or right side of the brain, that send messages of emotions to the heart, such as a heartache. These feelings are directed out of the right brain but are physically felt in the heart. In other words, our feelings are born in our head and then move to our heart.

Here are the distinct functions of the left side versus the right side of the brain. As you can see, they control very different aspects in our day-to-day lives.

The left brain is:

Analytical
Objective
Scientific
Logical
Rational
Intellectual
Realistic
Time bound

The right brain is:

Imaginative
Subjective
Artistic
Unconscious
Intuitive
Feeling
Internal
Emotional
Timeless

Whenever we learn something new, it goes directly into the left brain, where it is analyzed to see if it is important, is sorted out, and then is properly filed for later use. If at any time in the future we need to access any of the knowledge or information we have stored, as long as we are calm, the chemical serotonin begins to flow through a small tube to the left side of the brain. Serotonin acts as a secretary, locates and retrieves the information, and brings it to the forefront of our mind, enabling us to use that data to solve whatever problem or challenge we have at hand. This process takes place every time we consciously need information to problem solve; make a decision, big or small; or just recall information to have a conversation. As long as we remain in a state of emotional calm, that serotonin secretary stays busy supplying us with all the information we need to effectively problem solve and effectively live our lives.

However, if by chance we need that information to address a problem where any emotion is involved, whether frustration, anger, anxiety, fear, or any perceived or felt threat, fear of loss, or fear of any kind, a physical and neurological event takes place in the brain. The small tube that leads to the left brain begins to constrict and in extreme heightened cases, completely shuts down. The serotonin secretary can no longer travel to the left brain to acquire logical information to deal with our crisis and is therefore forced to detour into the right brain for its source of information, where we begin what is called the journey into our "emotional hijacking"!

An emotional hijacking occurs when you are faced with a perceived potential threat of any kind. When that takes place, the tube that leads directly to the left brain where all your logic is stored, which is the tube that the serotonin secretary travels to get the necessary information to make a productive decision, begins to tighten up or shrink; the larger the threat, the smaller and tighter the tube. The tighter the tube, the less access you have to your left brain. This forces you to travel to the emotional right side of the brain to solve your problem, as the left brain has been cut off. The greater the feeling and emotion, the tighter and smaller the tube to the left side of the brain becomes and the more it opens up to the right side of the brain. If the emotion is overwhelming with high levels of anger or fear involved, things can get seriously out of hand.

When a person incurs an emotional hijacking, he or she can be considered and described as going temporarily insane. An emotional hijacking originating in the brain, transitioning to the mouth, and even playing out in a person's actions or behavior can be the ultimate disaster for everyone involved.

When we allow negative emotions to control us, when we try to solve difficulty in our life using our right brain, we usually complicate and compound the problem. Emotional hijackings don't just occur with the major problems in our lives, they can occur with any daily problem where we are not getting our way or where we perceive ourselves to be potentially abused or taken advantage of.

Negative, emotion-based people are controlled by their right brain and become daily victims. They live a life of one tragedy after another. Their emotions control their decisions, rather than their logic controlling their destiny. Their perceptions of the world are victim-based, and their focus is always on the wrong thing. They constantly feel abused and their pain is so great, all they can think about is feeling better and being treated right. The feelings they hurt, the damage they do, or the price that has to be paid doesn't matter. Their demand for feeling better is stronger than an addictive drug.

Negative, Emotion-Based Traders

Negative, emotion-based people make terrible traders. They fail to look at things logically in life; therefore, if they become traders, they fail to look at the market logically. When they lose, they take it personally. After losing a few times, rather than having that positive attitude that is necessary to earn their money back, they become fearful and feel victimized, which places them in a position to eventually self-destruct, losing all their money. In the end they refuse to accept responsibility and blame the market, not themselves. Why? Because most emotion-based people live in denial, refuse to accept responsibility, and are more pessimistic about everything in life. It becomes almost impossible to learn new skills when one is filled with negative emotion, is frustrated, or is depressed.

> Negative, emotion-based people make terrible traders.

With the heart being controlled by the right side of the brain, or the emotional side of the mind, emotional traders are challenged to not use their hearts, but instead trade by using the charts. In other words, trade with no feeling.

It has been said that most people who live in poverty are heavily driven by their emotions when it comes time to making decisions about their life. People who live a life of mediocrity are somewhat split in using logic versus emotion in their decision-making processes. However, most people who live a life of success and manage their success are heavily left brained and use predominantly logic with only limited emotion when it comes time to making decisions about their life.

Emotional Trading

In a calm, emotional environment, the emotional and rational sides of the mind work in tight harmony with the sole focus of helping you achieve all levels of success in your life. It is imperative you understand that the rational and emotional sides of the mind are very independent, yet very distinct and individually strong. Usually there is a clear balance between the two as they interact constantly, working their way through every challenge and decision that is required daily.

From time to time, the rational side of the mind vetoes the influence of the emotional side of the mind, and vice versa. Even though the rational side of the mind can be logical and intelligent, when strong feelings or deep passion increase or surge, the emotional side of the mind begins to dominate all thought and the scale is tipped. The emotional side of the mind then takes control, demanding the subconscious mind to create actions based on its feelings or emotion.

Hence, when a trade is not properly planned out before execution, you are subject to an emotional hijacking if the market begins to move against you. With an emotional hijacking, the emotional side of the brain feels threatened and shouts out, "Emergency, emergency!" With that signal, it takes control of the rational side of the brain, not allowing it any time to evaluate the situation. The emergency summons the subconscious mind to create an immediate action to protect itself from the perceived danger.

This God-given mechanism can become critical to preserving life in a given situation or preserving your finances as you trade. If the market is racing against you, when an instant response is required to get out as fast as possible or in any way possible, then the instinctual emotional mind takes control. An irrational, delayed response could be devastating and wipe out your entire account.

The rational, logical side of the brain says to create a trading plan before you trade and then execute that plan. Yet you have a hunch, a feeling that the market is getting ready to explode, and you want in. That feeling or hunch overrides the logical side of the brain that says you need to create a trading plan before you trade. After you are in, you discover you were right: it was about to explode and it now has exploded, but in the opposite direction of your trade. You immediately feel danger. Alarms go off. Past experiences of massive losses immediately resurface. You feel threatened financially, so without any rational thought of where the market is, you immediately get out at a loss to protect yourself, only to find out the second you get out, the market bounces and takes off in your original desired direction. Why? Now that you are able to step back and walk through your trade with the rational side of the brain, you see that you entered when the market was perhaps consolidating right before it was going to take off, perhaps creating nothing more than a bull or bear trap, which ultimately scared the life out of you.

Because you entered based on emotion versus a rational and well-thought-out plan, when the market retraced further, it immediately scared you and you felt threatened, shocked, and fearful; all your past losses flashed in front of your face; and you said to yourself, "I am not going through this pain again and taking another financial loss." So you get out even if it means taking a small loss. Notice how your emotions controlled your actions. Your fear created a temporary emotional hijacking, and you crashed and burned.

How to Avoid Irrational and Emotional Trading

The only way to avoid such negative trading issues is to focus on a disciplined belief system that there is greater benefit in approaching trading with the rational left side of the brain versus the emotional right side of the brain. Life is nothing but a comedy for those who think about it and a real tragedy for those who feel their way through it.

> Life is nothing but a comedy for those who think about it and a real tragedy for those who feel their way through it.

I know people who wear their emotions on their sleeves, who are constantly feeling their way through life, and always end up the victims to what life has to offer. It becomes habit for them to use their emotions to think and problem solve. That mindset creates problem after problem for them in their life, whereas the opposite takes place for logical thinkers. A life of successful living is nothing more than realizing that our lives are filled with daily problems and the more effective we are at solving those problems in a state of logic, the happier we are and the more financially successful we become. Believe it or not, people who excel in math do well in life financially. It doesn't matter how you feel emotionally about math problems: five plus three will always equal eight.

The ability to properly reason with logic and limited emotion is extremely valuable. No doubt, positive emotions are a great asset in our lives. However, when it comes to daily problem solving and even trading, we must be totally aware of our emotions and be clear on how we will manage them, especially as we trade.

When emotions overwhelm concentration, the mind does not have access to the rational side of the left brain. It cannot reason or stay focused on the task at hand. Traders who are anxious, angry, frustrated, or depressed have a difficult time making good trading decisions or even learning how to trade. And as you would expect, people who are anxious, angry, frustrated, or depressed have a difficult time making good life decisions.

Seven Agreements

We can make the following seven agreements with ourselves to get our brain to work to our advantage instead of against us. After all, as traders we need to learn how to take advantage of the market instead of letting the market take advantage of us.

Think Only Positive Successful Thoughts as You Trade

Prepare yourself emotionally to succeed before you trade; envision succeeding. Your mind is the most powerful trading tool you will use. What we think about most as we trade will usually happen to us as we trade. If we dwell on negativity, on thoughts of defeat, of fear, and that trading is much too hard, or on thoughts of getting emotionally, mentally, and financially beat up, then it *will* be too hard and we *will* get financially beat up. People are meant to succeed and enjoy life, not fail. Failure comes to those who have not taken the time to figure out how things are meant to be. True failure is a state of mind. True success is the acceptance that failure is the process we must go through to become successful and that each failure takes us that much closer to becoming successful. One of the major struggles that people deal with on a daily basis is having a true assessment of ourselves, of our self-worth and self-esteem. We have been so beaten up by our past—from past hurts, failures, and situations that caused us pain—that we feel we are not worthy to become successful; therefore, we think negatively. We need to break the negativity spell and bring only optimistic thoughts of success to the trading table.

Destiny is not a matter of chance—it is a matter of choice; it is not a thing we wait for—it is a thing we consciously set out to achieve. As you begin your journey as a trader, you will either control your destiny or you will place it in the hands of someone else. There certainly is a lot to learn in life. But people who get ahead in life and really enjoy the most out of it are those who refuse to remain on the sidelines or to sit idle and do nothing, sighing and wishing things could be different. They neither complain of their lot in life, the hand they were dealt, nor their present circumstances. They don't waste time daydreaming or sitting around passively waiting for some distant ship to come in. Rather, they think positive, visualize their success, and chart a course to begin achieving it and making it a reality. They logically and verbally take a position in life and announce they are not emotional quitters. They refuse to succumb to life's negative circumstances. They decline to listen to any negative emotional voice that says, "You can't do that, you're a loser," or any voice that tries to hold them down, limit them, or rob them of their future. They logically realize that yesterday is a canceled check, tomorrow is a promissory note, and today is the only cash we have. Having this mindset, it becomes critical to keep the left side of your brain as accessible as possible so you can spend your cash wisely.

Keep It Simple

Commit to make whatever you do even simpler. Use your left brain to find straightforward, productive trading strategies that make sense and will yield a constant profit. Our lives are cluttered with too many facts and details that overwhelm and leave us in a state of negative overwhelmed emotion. Simply simplify. At first, trading can be very complicated and overwhelming, as there is a lot to learn. The best thing you can do is to slow down, be thorough, and try to understand as much as you can. Devote yourself to being a student. The more information you have about trading, the more options you will have. As you start to build a foundation of knowledge, everything will begin to fall into place, your understanding will broaden, and your personality will begin to gravitate toward something that will feel good, feel right and natural. As you experience that feeling, it is a sign your left brain and right brain are working in close harmony. Go after it. Simplicity, clarity, singleness: these attributes give traders power, vividness, and profitability.

Continue to Educate Yourself

Education's purpose is to replace an empty mind with information that creates an open mind. We are here to fill our left brain with as much information as we can to help us succeed in any way we can. With trading being 10 percent skill and 90 percent emotion, we have a responsibility to learn more about our emotions and how our right brain works with our left brain. We retain 10 percent of what we hear, 30 percent of what we read, 70 percent of what we do, but 100 percent of what we feel. Most of us hate dealing with emotions; however, with just a little education and practice on how to manage and merge our emotions with a simple trading methodology, our trading career can dramatically change for the better. And if we carry that education and awareness into our home life, it will enable us to move into a new phase of life so rewarding that hopefully we will be motivated to continue the education and self-improvement necessary to become better at what we do, and to ultimately becoming the best version of ourselves.

> You cannot teach a people anything; you can only help them find something within themselves and encourage them to bring it out.

You cannot teach a people anything; you can only help them find something within themselves and encourage them to bring it out. Change must come from within, not from your teacher. The beautiful part about learning is that no one can take it away from you, and the payoff is delicious in terms of improved quality of life and improved quality of trading ability. Keep your education simple. If you study to remember, you will forget; but if you study to understand, you will remember.

Replace a Bad Trading Habit with a Good One

Conquer your bad habits, or they will conquer you. A habit is either the best of servants or the worst of masters. Reread the opening page of this book. Replace a bad destructive habit with a constructive habit that enhances your life. Habit is overcome by habit. Only removing a bad habit leaves a void similar to a vacuum; it will look for something to draw into its place. Be intentional, and replace a bad practice with a good one immediately. Look into the mirror and be truthful. Are you everything you always wanted to be? Are your habits those of a person whom the world would rise for and admire? Are your trading habits those of a profitable, professional trader? Our character can be defined as a composite of our habits. We are what we repeatedly do. Excellence, then, is not a onetime event, it is a habit! It is not a single achievement, but rather a series of accomplishments. It involves building a track record of wins.

Don't Take Anything Personally While Trading

Don't let any offense stand in the way of where you are going. The world steps aside for people who know where they are going. Such people do not let little or even big things get in their way. They take nothing personally. Nothing can offend them. You can always tell the size of a person by the size of what offends that person. Small-minded people get upset over small things. Too many people stay focused on the wrong issue as they try to achieve a goal.

The world steps aside for people who know where they are going.

If your goal is to reach a target, you cannot afford to focus on the things or issues that stand in your way to the target. To do that takes the focus off the target and places it on the issue. That is a bad habit. As you move forward learning how to trade, you cannot let anything offend you or take anything personally. You cannot let this market offend you. You cannot let the broker offend you. Again, you cannot take anything personally. To take something personally takes the focus off your end goal.

Don't Assume Anything When You Trade

In life, we walk around assuming everything. When we wake up, we assume the coffee machine is going to work. We assume there will be hot water when we shower. We assume the chair we sit in is going to hold; we assume when we turn on our computer, it will work. We even assume that everything involved with our daily routine will exist, carry out its function, and be on time, and when it doesn't, it alters our mindset. Many times we incur emotional hijackings through our assumptions, and they take us down negative mental and emotional roads. Agreeing not to assume anything keeps you from presuming things are going great. Then we agree ahead of time not to suffer an emotional hijacking when something we thought was going great no longer is going great or when something that was to happen to our advantage has instead happened as a big disadvantage. Beg constantly for the bad news from everybody in your life. We all know how to act with good news, but to manage our lives successfully, we need to know the bad news as soon as possible to effectively use our left brains to resolve those issues. When bad news comes into our lives, it usually comes as a surprise, followed by an emotional hijacking, which does nothing more than place us in a position to create more problems for ourselves.

Do Your Best: Admit When You Make a Mistake and Move On

Real winners in life are the people who accept responsibility for their actions. They never focus on blaming anyone or anything. They accept that whatever happens or has happened is part of life's process. They are people who look at every situation with a belief and expectation that they can make it better. Having problems is not the problem. Problems are a part of life. But not paying attention to mistakes that create problems can become a problem. Making one mistake may be an accident. Making the same mistake twice may be a coincidence, but making the same mistake three times or more is a pattern. If properly addressed, a mistake that turns into a problem may ultimately give birth to an opportunity, an open door, a new way of thinking, or a newfound approach. We only have a problem when we believe in our minds that there are no clearly defined solutions to the problem. If you make a mistake, ante up. Don't run and hide, and don't make excuses for yourself. Unless you are a habitual offender, be happy that you are that much closer to success. No one is perfect, so do not create a false pretense to others of something that you are when you are not.

Conclusion

Remember that our brain is one of the most valuable assets and resources in our lives. Learn how to appropriate the merger of the left brain and right brain to your successful life's advantage. No one likes grumps and negative people—except other grumps and negative people. Think positive, think right, speak right, and act right so you will be all right. Believe that you can achieve and improve the merger of your left brain and right brain to your benefit as well as have fun as you attempt to do it. It will be reflected in the quality of your life and in your trading results. When you get your head and heart working in harmony, and your needs and wants operating in clear perspective, then your life begins to function at optimum levels of speed for success.

CHAPTER 6

THE IMPORTANCE
OF EMOTIONAL
INTELLIGENCE

It isn't what you don't know that will hurt you. It's what you think
you know but isn't so that ultimately destroys you. One of the
major missing parts for the ultimate success equation in trading,
and in life in general, is emotional intelligence. My research and
interaction with traders all over the world confirm that theory.
When traders begin to learn the skills of trading, they really don't
care much to talk about their emotions; however, after a couple
weeks of live trading, they suddenly start to care a lot about how
to handle their emotions while involved in the market. Perhaps for
the first time, they are introduced to the real emotions of fear and
greed, and in most cases they do not know how to respond effectively. When they win, they feel invincible, and when they lose,
they feel vulnerable and fearful. Either way, with time, most begin
to lose control of their emotions while in a trade and begin to self-
destruct. They understand the rules and disciplines of safeguarding
one's emotions yet disobey all of them when their emotions take
control of their actions. They also fail to realize the cause and effect
of these emotional actions.

Emotional intelligence is a state in which you exercise positive
self-control over negative, damaging emotions. Emotional intelligence allows you to tap into the right information within your
brain that gives you the discernment to engage the proper human
connections with the right influential people who will enhance

your life. At trading, emotional intelligence helps you tap into the appropriate information within your left brain that gives you the correct logical information, while severing ties to the right brain, which influences erratic, fearful, destructive, or negative actions. Staying tapped into the left brain during a trade will enhance your trading results.

When we are emotionally intelligent, we understand ourselves better and find it easier to interact with others. We recognize, understand, and choose how to think, feel, and act during a given situation. Traders have the responsibility of controlling themselves and their emotions while trading. Maintaining emotional control during the day directs many of our daily actions and allows us to set the right priorities in our lives. It defines who we are and participates in building our character. It allows us to do what is right and not act out how we feel. It also allows people to go to work and come home seeing the world differently.

The big question is, what is of greater value, academic intelligence or emotional intelligence? When it comes time for me to interview new potential members to the Market Traders Institute team, I am more interested in their emotional intelligence than I am in their intellectual intelligence. Why? I can teach them just about any skill we do here at work rather rapidly; however, it is painstakingly laborious to teach anyone emotional intelligence. This is because emotional intelligence has to do with naturally formed, subconscious, automatic responses to situations where the individual feels emotionally attacked or faced with a problem.

I would rather know how they respond to and deal with situations, how they process things, how they go about problem solving, and how they work through and resolve conflict—all of which are *essential* to succeeding as a trader. Our work responsibilities and much of life are really about effective problem solving. Every day presents us with potential opportunities that can enhance our lives but also are more than likely accompanied by many problems. As we go about trying to take advantage of these countless opportunities, we have no choice but to try to work through the snags that arise. How we go about working through those surprises determines whether we are emotionally intelligent or emotionally unintelligent.

> You can alter your life, attitude, destiny, and trading
> results by understanding emotional intelligence.

Loving to Trade and Handling Your Emotions

In the scientific sense, emotions act as a gauge, a guide, a plumb line. They act as a compass, pointing us in the right direction, enabling human beings to experience joy, happiness, passion, and love. An emotion takes place when certain biological, experiential, and cognitive states occur simultaneously in the brain. Certain biological changes take place in the brain when the feeling of happiness is present in the mind. There is an increase of activity in a brain center that inhibits negative feelings by fostering a surplus of energy on standby. Feelings of love immobilize fear and anger. Love generates a state of calm and contentment. If fear and anger are enemies to traders when trading, doesn't it make sense for traders to place themselves in a position of loving their trading careers? With novice traders, their fear being one of the major emotional components driving their decisions in the market, it would be well advised to understand what is taking place in the brain to achieve mental clarity and success as they trade.

Effectively managing our emotions increases intuition and clarity. Traders need intuition and clarity before, during, and after a trade. Letting our emotions run wild can destroy potentially productive outcomes in our personal lives, and if they are left alone to run wild, they can and will destroy our trading outcomes and trading destiny. Choosing to control and constructively handle our emotions helps us self-regulate our brain chemicals and internal hormones. Learning to master our emotions is the real foun-

dation for clarity and the enjoyment of life. It brings a newfound
freedom.

Recognizing the Power and Importance of Emotional Intelligence

The Center for Creative Leadership wrote in 1994 that "75 percent
of careers are derailed for reasons related to emotional incompetence, including inability to handle interpersonal problems; unsat-
isfactory team leadership during times of difficulty or conflict;
or inability to adapt to change or elicit trust."[1] In other words, it
is far better to be emotionally intelligent . . . than intellectually
intelligent!

For the first time in history, major corporations, managers,
leaders, and coaches are taking into consideration the emotional
intelligence of an individual as a critical factor in high levels of
leadership. World-leading organizations are adopting the practices
of educating their people about emotional intelligence and adopting it into their organizational development and human resources.

John Gottman, a Ph.D. who studies emotional intelligence
stated, "In the last decade or so, science has discovered a tremendous amount about the role emotions play in our daily lives and
work lives. Researchers are coming to the conclusion and have
found that even more than IQ, your emotional awareness and abilities to handle feelings will determine your success and happiness
in all walks of life, including family relationships."[2]

The world needs to incur a paradigm shift enabling it to start
thinking and understanding that all emotions—love, apprecia-

1. Margaret Meloni, "What Is EQ and Why Should You Care?" Pickthe
   brain.com, http://www.pickthebrain.com/blog/what-is-eq-and-why-should
   -you-care. July 2009.
2. John Gottman, Ph.D., *Raising an Emotionally Intelligent Child: The Heart of
   Parenting.* Simon and Schuster: New York, 1998, p. 20.

tion, anger, or anxiety—are energies that have to be accounted for because they create actions, whether actions of love or of retaliation. Each of us is personally accountable for the cause and effect of our emotions, attitudes, and actions. Negative emotional energies wreak havoc on our own lives as well as the lives we touch, and in the end will often cause mental, emotional, and physical disorders. Traders who are controlled by their negative actions as they trade ultimately never make it.

By applying emotional intelligence to almost all problems or issues in your personal life as well as in trading, you can see more clearly in the direction you need to go to stop your self-defeating behavior. If you can begin to get into the habit of recognizing when a situation or circumstance triggers your emotions to default to a downward spiral, and you observe that an emotional hijacking may be starting, then you have already crossed the first bridge. Recognition and awareness are the first step. What you do next is critical. Now is the time to pause and think before speaking; or, better yet, if you have time to remove yourself from the situation and return once you have come up with a well-thought-through answer or position, you will start to see a noticeable difference in your life for the better.

As traders begin to habitually recognize their negative emotions and shift what is taking place inside those negative emotions to positive actions, their trading takes a 180-degree turn. Each success at effective problem solving will build more self-confidence and assurance and lead to excitement and enthusiasm at the trading table.

When long-standing emotional issues start to lose some of their intensity and importance in your life and they stop bothering you as much, the end result will be a new level of insight, which can give you a brand-new vantage point into your personal life and trading life. I have seen and even heard of many traders grabbing their computers during a trade gone bad and throwing it to the wall or ground, only to realize that they are still in the trade. They then panic even more because they have to find a phone and the broker's number to get out of the trade, as the market is racing against them.

If we lack emotional intelligence, the human brain switches to autopilot whenever stressful situations arise and has an inherent tendency to quickly and automatically respond to fight or flight, which more often than not is exactly the wrong approach in solving the majority of today's problems. While strong right-brain feelings can create either chaos or caution in the left brain (caution is a good thing to have, and it's not always smart to abandon your caution), the lack of awareness of your conscious feelings can also be disastrous and have you override your logical reasoning.

Emotional Intelligence in a Trader's Life

The reality is that there is no thinking without feeling and no feeling without thinking. The two work in unison. Logic alone cannot be used for certain decisions, such as deciding whom to marry, whom to trust, or even what job to take or career path to embark on. Heavy decisions like this can be multifaceted and complex. They can become devastating if logic and feeling are not merged properly to discern.

People who were deathly afraid to talk about their emotions are beginning to talk about emotions for the first time in their lives, especially male traders. For the first time in the workplace or in trading clubs, they are becoming familiar with their emotions and are opening up by listening, understanding, and extending empathy, which is really making a difference in their home dynamics, the workplace, and their trading results. If in life or at trading you cannot control your emotions, detect when your emotions are changing, or express empathy, *then no matter how smart you are, you are not going to get very far.*

Trading is all about emotional intelligence. It is about entering into a trade and keeping access to your left brain completely open. Logic is the oxygen and life to the trader, while uncontrolled emotion is its death! When you trade by your heart instead of the chart, you are finished!

> If you cannot control your emotions, no matter how smart you are, you are not going to get very far.

No doubt, decisions we make while trading in the market affect our ego, whether positively or negatively. Depending on our results, the more positive the outcome, the better we feel about ourselves, and the smarter we think ourselves to be. The opposite is also true. The more negative the outcome of our decisions, the worse we feel about ourselves, and the dumber we think ourselves to be. We can begin to perceive ourselves as a loser trader, and our ego takes a hit.

The fact is, our identity is attached to situations and circumstances and affects how we think and feel when we problem solve in life and at trading. We also have the added pressure that everyone is watching. Our actions are an extension of our thoughts and feelings. Usually when we feel anger, we allow ourselves to become angry and think on anger's terms. Our acting out then shows the world who we truly are. We become anger itself. Whatever begins in anger ends in shame. When we feel depressed, we think on depression's terms, we act depressed, we become depressed; and our actions show the world who we are. When we feel greedy, the same process takes place and we become greedy. The true sign of an intelligent person is the ability to control emotions through the application of reason, whenever these feelings arise. Whenever any negative feeling starts to present itself, rid yourself of it as quickly as possible.

Our main search then is to find ourselves emotionally and to be reborn, to embrace our calling, to reach our highest potential, and become all that we can be in this life, all the while touching and enhancing the lives of others. This is a search to be reborn emotionally, to start a new life. No one can go back in time to change anything, but we can all move forward, emotionally reborn with intelligent habits that bless lives rather than curse, hurt, or damage them.

The most important outcome and greatest reward for all our efforts of implementing emotional intelligence is a safe reputation, that is, constantly protecting and building a character that is truly great. Possessing a skill is easy, but the execution of it is what tells the world who and what we are. Emotional intelligence is the foundation to successful living. When successful traders solve problems, they direct their emotions and don't let their emotions direct them. Because they steer clear of such obstacles, they are happy traders.

> Emotional intelligence is the foundation to successful living.

So much of our happiness and success begins with not only understanding how things work, but understanding concepts and principles that you can apply and put into practice. And ultimately you can make subconscious habits of those actions and develop your character.

A Trader's Relationship with the Market

When you think with the end in mind, the conscious and unconscious parts of the brain begin working in unison to save the relationship. When it comes time to trading, who do you have a relationship with? The market! You want your relationship to last, don't you? After all, the only way you can profit or benefit from the market is by engaging and being involved. The only way you can benefit from a relationship is by being involved. Human relationships are about giving and taking, and your relationship with the market is about give and take as well.

When you care about a human relationship or a connection you have made, you are willing to do all kinds of things to understand the person and work through specific problems to preserve the relationship, because you believe that relationships have value. I know people who truly believe they do not need anyone or any relationship to survive, because they believe it is sometimes too costly, emotionally and financially, to maintain long-term relationships. Those who value friendships or relationships think and feel differently; they see and enjoy the benefits.

Likewise, if you care enough about your relationship with the market, you will be willing to do all kinds of things to work through the relationship, enabling it to last and enjoying the profits you can derive from it. Too many traders try to force the market to do what they want it to do and end up losing all their money. Actually, it is a trader's responsibility to first seek to understand what the market is capable of doing before getting involved.

A Trader's Responsibility to Emotional Intelligence

Let me help you understand in greater detail the responsibility of traders to have ownership of their emotional intelligence as they trade. I teach our clients who are learning to trade that the market is never wrong—it is always right. It is the trader who is sometimes right and sometimes wrong. With those odds stacked against traders, they have a greater responsibility to learn how to position themselves on the right side of the market as it moves.

The market is never wrong—it is always right.

A fundamental piece of knowledge on learning to trade is learning the simple concept that the market can do only two things: move up or down. That is it! As it is moving up or down, traders can learn and apply several strategies, enabling them to take advantage of the market. I always ask traders, "If you were taught where to get into the market and why, and where to get out of the market and why, do you think you could make some money?" The answer is always yes.

I then ask myself, "Why do so many people self-destruct after being taught where to get in the market and why, and where to get out and why?" The answer is lack of emotional intelligence! It is the lack of self-awareness, of not knowing yourself.

Our mind is vital to our body. Without the mind, the body is of no use. But if programmed correctly, the mind can become one of our greatest assets. If programmed incorrectly or left to fend for itself, it becomes one of our greatest liabilities. Part of learning and implementing emotional intelligence is dissecting and understanding how we came to feel a certain way. Have you ever wondered why it is that two people can witness the same situation and walk away with two totally different views as to what happened? Or you and your partner can watch the same movie and yet later retell the story so differently?

The fact is, we are all the result of our past programming. Some say we are all victims of our past programming. I say we are all either victims or benefactors of our past programming. The difference between the two is in the way you choose to see it. If you are used to seeing yourself as a victim, you can change your way of thinking to become a victor instead. That choice becomes yours.

Our minds have consciously and subconsciously recorded all of life's lessons and experiences, and they now influence our daily actions. Our thoughts become our actions, and our actions become our character.

Executing the Trade: The Conscious and Subconscious Minds

Here is the law of the conscious and subconscious minds: whatever you consciously think about in a repetitive nature, your subconscious will automatically take over and create the self-fulfilling action to match the thought. Your subconscious mind is not going to try to prove that whatever you are thinking about is good or bad, true or false; rather it is only going to respond by creating an action to match what you habitually think about.

When you begin to actually execute a trade for the first time, your conscious mind is thinking through every step of the way, while your subconscious mind is recording every single action along the way, like grabbing your trade checklist, drawing trend lines on the charts, opening up your trading platform, or taking the mouse and executing a trade of buying and selling. The subconscious mind records all the actions executed while doing the task. The conscious mind does the actions that require thinking and deciding where to get in the market.

The conscious mind thinks, and the subconscious mind acts. As you walk through the trade step-by-step thinking about it for the very first time, your actions are being recorded by your subconscious mind. Why? It enables that action to be ready the next time you consciously think about it in the future. That is the relationship between the conscious and subconscious minds. That is why the conscious mind is the gatekeeper for the subconscious mind. You do not want to think about and do bad things and form bad habits.

The critical part about this process of forming habits is that once the conscious mind accepts an idea, concept, value, or moral and determines that it is agreeable, it begins to think about it and creates an inclination. The more that thought is accessed, regurgitated, and acted on, it becomes an action that the subconscious mind records. Once the past action is thought about for the second time by the conscious mind and acted out by the subconscious mind, then thought about and acted out a third time, and repeated enough times, it becomes a habit, good or bad.

The subconscious mind doesn't know the difference between good and bad, right or wrong, fair or unfair, just or unjust—it only knows action and habit. Think good and positive thoughts, and the subconscious mind will look through all its past recorded files and get you to act out good and positive actions. Think bad and negative thoughts, and the subconscious mind will look through all of its past recorded files and get you to act out bad and negative actions. That is the power of thinking, and the reason why we need to control our thoughts.

Successful trading is all about winning on your trade *before you even execute the trade.* If before you sit down at your computer to trade, you can envision yourself being that successful trader and think, "I am a successful trader, I am good at what I do, and I will win at my trading today," then your subconscious mind will call to the forefront all your past successes and direct you to execute only actions from your past successful trades. However, if you let just one ounce of negative thought to get involved and you start thinking negative, fearful, and doubtful loser thoughts and that you are going to lose on the trade, your subconscious mind will call up all your past recorded bad actions that accompanied your losses and failures and force you to execute only those losing actions.

For whatever you habitually let your mind dwell on, your subconscious mind will create habitual actions that become self-fulfilling prophecies of the original thoughts. Learn to meditate on the positive thoughts. Meditate, you ask? If you know how to worry, you already know how to meditate. Worry is about meditating on negative thoughts, negative outcomes, and negative results. Practice meditating on positive thoughts, positive outcomes, and positive results. Take time to envision yourself succeeding. I cannot emphasize this enough: I have seen traders' careers totally turned around just from altering their thoughts. I have seen traders make up all their losses just by changing their thought patterns. So if you say to yourself before you trade, "I hate trading! Every time I trade, I lose," or "Every time I take a position in the market, it goes against me,"—well, guess what you are doing? You are self-sabotaging! Why and how? In the past, your subconscious mind actually recorded the step-by-step past events where you lost in that trade. And you have thought about that event so much, your subconscious mind has become really clear on what needs to be done to repeat that event. Believe in failure, and it will happen. Believe in success in life or at trading, and that will happen.

I cannot emphasize this enough: I have seen traders' careers
totally turned around just from altering their thoughts.

Conclusion

Choosing to display emotional intelligence, or emotional unintelligence, can make the difference between living out a life of poverty and mediocrity or one of great success. What we think about is what we do, and what we do tells the world who we are!

Your emotional intelligence will prove more important in your trading life than your intellectual intelligence will. Emotional intelligence is not only an introduction to how we should be thinking and acting to find financial success, but also an understanding that gives people permission to feel, that is, a structure for bringing their emotional lives into the workplace. It is a new sort of language. It also prompts people to think before they speak and think before they act, suggesting a shift in perspective when problem solving.

Don't underestimate the incredible responsibility of the conscious mind. It is to determine right from wrong. It is to determine what is good for us and what is bad for us as we search for any kind of success in this life. The conscious mind is the protective guard of the subconscious mind; it should let only good thoughts pass to the subconscious mind, which in turn should form only good habits. The conscious mind's sole function is to protect the subconscious mind from receiving erroneous, untruthful, or unhealthy information that will create a harmful, destructive habit. Remember, the subconscious mind cannot determine good from bad, right from wrong, success from failure. It only acts out what the conscious mind relentlessly thinks about. Think success, and success follows. Think failure, and failure follows.

CHAPTER 7

THE IMPORTANCE OF CHANGE

If you are living paycheck to paycheck, your spending is out of control, you are barely getting by, you possess no assets, and you are swamped with debt, then you are probably involved with managing your poverty. If you are living within your means, have a budget, control your spending, possess few or no assets, have a small amount in savings, and are slowly paying off your debt, you are probably managing your mediocrity. If you are living within your means, allocate your finances appropriately, possess assets with little or no debt, and aggressively grow your investment or savings, you are probably managing your success.

You cannot find success—it must find you. It is like a magnet and is attracted only to its equivalent! If you are not like success . . . it will refuse to stick around. There was a time in my life when all I did was look for success. The harder I looked for it, the further it seemed to run away and hide. After wondering for years why I could not find it, it dawned on me that perhaps I had the concept of finding success all backward. Perhaps instead of trying to be attracted to it, I needed to place myself in a position for it to be attracted to me.

You cannot find success—it must find you.

So I looked up *success* in a dictionary to see if I was the type of person success would be attracted to. It's defined as:

- An event that accomplishes its intended purpose
- An attainment that is successful
- A state of prosperity or fame
- An achiever; a person with a record of successes ("only winners need apply"; "if you want to be a success, you have to dress like a success")
- A person of integrity

I thought to myself, that doesn't sound like me. Let me break it down further:

- An event that accomplishes its intended purpose—I don't even have a purpose yet.
- An attainment that is successful—I haven't attained much of anything.
- A state of prosperity or fame—I have no money to speak of and definitely no fame.
- An achiever; a person with a record of successes ("only winners need apply"; "if you want to be a success, you have to dress like a success")—I try to achieve, but I don't have a record of successes. I can't apply, because I'm not a real winner. And I certainly don't dress like success.
- A person of integrity; in psychology, this is referred to as "ego integrity"—I am still struggling with being a person of integrity, and I certainly don't have ego integrity.

The more I thought about all this, the more I knew I had to change so that success would be attracted to me when it came by. I kept asking myself, "But change how?" I needed to change in thought, speech, and action. I needed to clean up my thoughts and change the way I thought about things. I needed to change my speech, to start talking like a successful person, and to quit acting like an ignorant, immature fool. I had to start saying things of substance or decline to say anything at all. If I did say something, it had to be of value. If I opened my mouth and committed to or promised anything, I would need to ante up and do it, or shut up. Further, my actions needed to be honorable, respectful, and based on integrity. I needed to change by learning the habits of successful people so I could think, speak, and act like them, enabling success to be attracted to me and stick around when it came around.

No matter how hard you try, if you keep repeating your negative habits, you will never find success, because it will always be fleeting. Changing and fixing those negative habits preserves your character and integrity and creates a good reputation. When a good reputation is created for you, people tell all their friends about you and how they can trust you and feel safe with you—then success comes knocking at your door. All of a sudden you don't have to keep trying so hard to find success because it comes and finds you.

Has success found you? Do you need to change a few things in your life to allow success to find you and stick around?

Changing to Attract Success

Most people really don't understand the importance of change in their lives. They underestimate their need for it or question their ability to change. There is no better time than today to make a new start. No doubt, change is difficult, for people are by nature creatures of habit. If you wait for the right time to initiate a change, you may find that you will never begin.

People who are not experiencing success on a daily basis or achieving overall success in their life slowly become unhappy. Unhappy people fear change the most. Yet change is critical to attract success and eventually become happy.

Unhappy people fear change the most.

If you don't like where you are going in life or the way your world is, you have two choices: Keep on keeping on, living in your poor wretched state, a little blob of ailments; or muster up the courage to change your situation from being a victim to being a victor. I personally believe if you are not achieving your highest potential in this life, you are missing out on so many things that are just waiting to fall in your lap and would change your life for the better. You have an obligation to yourself, that is, your future personal happiness, your health, and your future security, to alter your outlook on life and not let this opportunity pass you by. If you are unhappy with something, change it; if you can't change it, change the way you look at and think about it!

To grow and mature in this life, we have to learn the art of changing and evolving. As one would expect, this involves risk. Taking risks requires stepping outside of our comfort zone. Life wouldn't be called a journey if everything was handed to you, if you were spoon-fed, and if there were no surprises or if all the unknowns were made known.

The only thing constant in this life is change. It is personal growth and development that become optional in our lives. It is a decision that only we can make; no one can make it for us. The moment we make that decision is the moment the world steps aside, allowing us to accomplish our goals and partake of the fruits of life. The quest for self-improvement and maturity or greatness is life-long. It is not a flippant decision we make one day, but a resolution we have every day, perhaps even renewing our commitment several times a day, if necessary. It is a mindset, a direction we choose, a voyage on which we embark. And the day we think we arrive, believing we are done changing, is the day we are truly finished and stop growing.

Small changes can make big differences. I have observed a shared habit of most successful people: if they begin their day every morning mapping out their vision for the day, clearly understanding what their objective is, and strategizing how they are going to achieve it, they make small changes daily. As a rule, before they get started on

THE IMPORTANCE OF CHANGE

any project, they enter into a research mode, seeking to obtain as much information as possible because it gives them options.

You must possess the talent of a chameleon: to be able to change and adapt rather quickly to new situations, environments, or challenges. Life is all about change. Change is the natural course of life. Think about it, we don't stay infants forever, do we? We learn to walk and talk, learn natural laws and basic concepts, and hopefully throughout our adult lives still learn, discover, and grow. Sometimes we don't think we have changed all that much, until we take the time to pause and reflect. Sometimes change is a slow-moving object in our lives that creeps all around us, letting its presence be known and felt only after it has left.

Look back at your life a year ago: what has changed? Look at the situation you were in. Look at how you worked through that situation and how it slowly changed you. We, hopefully, are not the same person this year as last year. Everything in this life is connected to preserve stability in our lives, to create a structure for survival or for success. Change is a part of that structure and will always be inevitable. There is nothing wrong with change and nothing to fear in change but rather everything to gain. The human life doesn't fear change so much as the unknown. Change is the essence of life, and to keep up with life, we must adapt, evolve, and be willing to sacrifice who we are for who we need to become. Always remember that good is the enemy of great.

Goals should be called processes. A goal implies finality when achieved, yet when we achieve a goal, we look to change the end result for the better and create an even bigger or better goal. Every time I set a goal and think I accomplished it, things change. It is a little like the technology era we are experiencing right now. By the time a new computer is finally manufactured, it is already outdated.

If we don't create the change we need, tailored for the betterment of our lives, change will create it for us, but it may not be the change we really want. As people go about their journey, shifting and making small adjustments along the way, life happens and inevitably brings hurdles and obstacles. Those setbacks can and will create discomfort. How prolonged is the question. This depends on our courage and willingness to keep fighting for the positive changes we so desperately need in our lives. Nobody can go back in time for a new beginning, but anyone can start making a new ending today.

Looking Back to Look Forward

If you are currently trading and not acquiring the success you were looking for, what are you going to do about it?

Look back over the last five years and ask if you are totally satisfied with the changes you have made in your life. Have things changed for the better or worse? Why? Then find a piece of paper and do the following: Take a moment to look back over the last year. Consider what you have done, what happened, and where you have succeeded or failed. Then write down three changes you consciously made that have benefited your emotional or financial life:

1. _____

2. _____

3. _____

Next, look back at your life over the past *five* years and write down three changes you consciously made that have had a significant impact for the betterment of your life.

1. _____

2. _____

3. _____

Now look at your list and ask yourself the question: Why did I change? Consider what will happen in the upcoming year, and write down three changes you want to make that you believe will enhance your life. It may even be something you tried to do before but was unable to accomplish. Next to each change, write down why you think you want to make that specific change.

Things I Want to Change   **Why?**

1. _____   _____

2. _____   _____

3. _____   _____

Now look forward five years, and write down five changes you think you will need to make to improve your financial and emotional situation.

Things I Want to Change   **Why?**

1. _____   _____

2. _____   _____

3. _____   _____

4. _____   _____

5. _____   _____

We were created to be happy, reach our highest potential, and enjoy a life of abundance, both financially and emotionally. If you are not experiencing a life of financial and emotional abundance, you have to ask yourself why. By dissecting your answer, you should find what you are looking for, and no matter what that is, it will involve change in your life.

If you are not experiencing a life of financial and
emotional abundance, you have to ask yourself why.

Most people fear change and are reluctant or unwilling to embrace it because it involves implementing a new behavior. We hate that. We think, "I like me just the way I am." But do you really? If you did, you would have nothing on your preceding list.

Why and How to Change

Why, then, does a person really change? What brings it about? Usually the desire for change is born in the cradle of dissatisfaction with something in our lives. We are frustrated; we are not where we thought we would be at this point in our lives. We are frustrated with our job, our marriage, our family dynamics, our neighborhood, our house, our car, our finances. We begin to become consciously aware of our misery and think, "Is this all I can expect out of life for the rest of my life?" That moment of awareness and despair creates a desire for change. The second step is admitting that we are miserable and that we do not want to stay that way.

Most people don't become miserable in one day. It is a process that happens over time. It is sad to see the mindset of people who have worked their way into a life of frustration or misery. The more stubborn and miserable they become, the more their minds reject change.

As I previously discussed, one of the first steps to achieving financial success in life and trading is the recognition that we are not succeeding in the manner we thought we would. That detection of our current status is called *conscious incompetence*. You are aware of your lack of success in whatever endeavor you embarked on. You are either miserable or frustrated, you are longing for a change, and you now admit it. You say to yourself, "I need change because I am not happy," or "I'm frustrated," or "I'm not very successful at what I am doing. I am locked in a series of unconscious incompetent, nonproducing, or destructive actions that have turned into bad habits, and I need to change that!"

That is the point when we need to get help. Most people, believe it or not, don't know how to get the appropriate help. The tragedy is that the majority of the world attacks this problem the wrong way. They think all they need to do is change their circumstances, such as getting a new job or acquiring a new work skill. I bet that may be why you came to learn about trading: you want to make a lot of money and change a few things in your life. Perhaps you are trying to get a fresh outlook on life, a new start. Well, I hate to be the bearer of bad news, but the reality is that all those unconscious incompetent habits you walk around with every day, like impatience, hot temperament, lack of anger-management skills, and impulsive destructive behaviors such as blaming, acting before thinking, not planning before implementing, "poor me" negative attitudes—basically, a victim mentality—will obstruct you from becoming the successful person you are so desperately trying to become in your career or at trading.

Change must be seen as an opportunity to make your life and situation better, not worse. People are won over by change when they see a greater benefit in doing something new versus something they presently do.

Changing from Unconscious Incompetence to Unconscious Competence

One of the exercises I walk through with traders who are losing money in the market is the unconscious incompetence–unconscious competence exercise. As human beings change, they go through the following metamorphic steps or process:

1. From unconscious incompetence
2. To conscious incompetence
3. To conscious competence
4. To unconscious competence

Step 1, unconscious incompetence, is the recognition you are going nowhere in your life and you are not very thrilled with where you are at or the actions taking place, if any, to change your current situation.

Step 2, conscious incompetence, is to look in the mirror and admit that what you are doing in your life is not working and you need help. If you are involved with repeating bad, unconscious, unproductive habits that leave you in a state of frustration, misery, and financially just getting by, then the only way your life is going to get better is if you consciously start to make it better.

Step 3, conscious competence, is to learn a new skill that can make things better in your life. When you learn a new skill for improvement, you go through the process I call conscious competence. Conscious competence can be defined as thinking about everything that needs to be done, step by step, and done right so your subconscious mind can record every action. Conscious competence is acquiring a new productive skill that will change things in your life for the better.

Step 4, unconscious competence, is to practice over and over the new productive skill you just learned that will enhance your life. Practice does not make perfect, it makes habit. You must practice that productive skill repeatedly until your subconscious mind takes over and you can execute that new productive skill without even thinking about it.

Walking through the four steps is a little like learning how to drive a car. After your subconscious mind nicely records all the steps, it eventually takes over and you do the task with little or no thought by your conscious mind. When you can do that, you have entered into unconscious competence. If you were to think about your driving habits today, you would probably admit you are unconsciously competent in that skill. You don't even need to think about the task of driving, because it has become an unconscious skill of competence. Successful people learn unconscious skills of competence that make them successful.

When people are at work and want to become successful, they consciously repeat productive skills over and over with discipline until they become unconscious productive habits. Those habits become the foundation for success. People who do this don't even need to think about the things they are doing, because they took the time to learn the skills of success and can perform them in an unconscious state.

Don't Tell the World What You Can Do—Show It

Change starts when someone sees the next step. So I am going to help you see the next step for the needed change in your life and in trading, enabling success to find you and stick around. Get your paper out again, and let's continue becoming students of change. There are six steps that help a person change for the better. If you really want to understand yourself, try to change yourself. If you really want to understand something, try to change it. Change can be hard for some people. Consider how hard it is to change others, and maybe you will understand why change is so difficult for everyone.

> If you really want to understand yourself, try to change yourself.

If you really want to change something that is not working in your life, the following six steps will help you move from conscious incompetence to unconscious competence—a life of unconscious success:

1. **Understand the benefit of change.** Look at your current habit that you want to change, and ask yourself what would be the benefits in your life if you changed this action. Maybe while you are trading you are feeling stressed, anxious, tempted, frustrated, and all those emotions result in impulsive, financially unsound, self-destructive emotional decisions. What would happen if you were calm and clearheaded? If you could avoid the stress and frustration?

2. **Dissect the proposed change and benefit.** Convince yourself that things in your life will become better if you change. Be

clear not only about what you want to change but also how you will go about it.

3. **Recognize the setup or situation that triggers your self-defeating or self-destructive action.** Consider those all-too-familiar conditions or circumstances that lend themselves to activating negativity within you and how you can consciously recognize them during the day when they happen. What systems and processes can you implement to avoid letting that situation become emotional?

4. **Create new habits so that when triggered, the fresh way of thinking and behaving will begin to override the latter.** Now we need to identify and implement the new action. Think about what this would be for you in each situation you considered in the previous step. For example, suppose by default your negative habit while trading is to worry that if you don't just get in the market quickly, you will miss out on a great opportunity. Yet you recognize that by impatiently chomping at the bit and not waiting for the right setup, you may presumptuously rush into a bad trade. Knowing this, recognize the rising emotion of stress or anxiety connected with feeling like you are missing out, consciously remind yourself that there is no such thing as the trade of the century and that a day has more than 1,000 trading opportunities—this isn't the only one.

5. **Practice removing and replacing those thought processes and habits: out with the old, in with the new.** Rehearse them over and over in your mind. Play out hypothetically what you will do when the situation arises. As you rehearse the rules, that is, the new policy you have implemented, envision yourself executing your new behavior. When it comes to trading, rehearse your new thought processes, walking through the actions step by step in your mind. Do this over and over until your mind accepts it and embraces it. Before you know it, it will be a routine action you carry out with ease.

6. **Commit openly to other people that you are making a change.** There is power in making a commitment out loud, by

saying it verbally. Declaring to the world what you are determining to do will create a greater personal commitment. It strengthens your resolve. Once you take a position with a new action and verbalize it, other people will participate in holding you accountable. They will act as coaches, pushing you to do better or cheerleaders encouraging and cheering you on.

Conclusion

We cannot change our past, but we can change our future. No doubt, some things are out of our control. We cannot change the fact that some people are just going to act a certain way that is going to cause us discomfort or create a major inconvenience, or that a surprise situation will create some sort of ripple effect. But we do have control over ourselves and how we respond to those people and events. We get to choose the way we look at things and change the way we respond to the unexpected. Like I said at the beginning of this chapter, many times things don't change, we just need to change the way we look at them, taking that information and working it to our advantage. That is all there is to it.

At times it seems that life reveals its answers about our destiny at its own pace, not at ours. You feel like running, but life only lets you jog. As life begins to reveal your destiny and you don't like it, you better start to change it. Otherwise things can change for the worse automatically if they are not altered for the better consciously. Don't forget: when human beings do not take the time to map out where they want to go, they have a self-preserving default mechanism setting labeled "SURVIVE." We will all eventually survive, if we don't take action for our destiny. Is that what you want? After all, destiny is not a matter of chance, it is a decision.

As you learn to trade, you will learn the market is not going to change. It is amazing how traders constantly blame the market for their lack of success. They say, "Well, the market has changed recently." No, it hasn't; that is an uneducated answer.

Destiny is not a matter of chance, it is a decision.

I have been observing this market on a daily basis for more than 20 years and have studied charts as far back as 50 years. The fact of the matter is that it hasn't changed one bit. It still goes up, down, and sideways, just as it always has. What changes in the market is our ability or inability to analyze it, interpret it, make a judgment call, and take a winning position.

Be the change you want to see in the world, even if that change is the slow-moving object in your life that makes things better. And whatever you do, *do not fear change!* Where fear controls, significant change becomes impossible. Don't forget:

Fear imprisons, change liberates.
Fear paralyzes, change empowers.
Fear disheartens, change encourages.
Fear sickens, change heals.
Fear makes us useless, change makes us useful.

Be the change you need to see in the market, and be the change you need to see in your life.

CHAPTER 8

CREATING A PERSONAL AND TRADER'S CONSTITUTION

Weakness of character creates weakness of destiny. Creating a constitution is the act or process of composing, setting up, or establishing a structure of performance, governed by a set of fundamental rules, laws, and principles that describe the nature, functions, and limits of one's performance. A constitution is a guide that should never be abandoned, regardless of the situation. It is not something to be taken lightly, but rather should be well thought out. It should not be written in sand, to be washed away with every new wave of enticement that comes along; rather, it should be carefully written and not easily changed. The U.S. Constitution, for example, was created and written not only for the current generation but for all posterity; a timeless document for its successors and descendants. There is no power in and of the text or paper itself; however, the power is in the written words that create a position in life. If we don't stand for something, we have the potential to fall for anything. A constitution is a reminder of a foundation you have promised to begin building your life and character on. Most successful people I have met have their own personal constitutions.

A trader's constitution also is governed by a set of fundamental rules, laws, and principles that describes the nature of your performance. It is a disciplined set of rules and laws that you are willing to obey. Once these laws and rules are established, obeying them will eventually participate in creating or changing your personality and will become part of your character.

What is character? Character is the inherent compilation of attributes that determines a person's moral and ethical actions and conduct. In other words, our character is all about what we do versus what we say. It is doing the right thing when no one we know is looking. It is the total sum of all our choices that turn into actions.

Character and Intellect

Our reputation is what everyone thinks of us, but our character is what we do and what we really are. A solid, moral character is more important than any God-given talent. We build it slowly, piece by piece, thought by thought, choice by choice, action by action. Character involves more than just possessing intellect. Intellect is the collection and compilation of learned information we gather throughout our life. Character is the art of combining intellect with the understanding and comprehension of how to properly appropriate our intellect in life. Character consists of many components. A few examples include:

- Knowing when to speak up and when to shut up
- Saying the right thing at the right time for the right reason
- Possessing sensitivity and creativity with which you problem solve
- What you do with knowledge and actions when no one is looking
- How you behave when you get confused or lost in life
- How you react to a state of fear or crisis

Most people think education and knowledge make character, but they are wrong. Character is a strong conviction to a set of values and rules that you have decided to follow and live by, regardless of how you feel. It is choosing to live by principle, not by feeling. It is having your armor on, ready at all times, so that when an ethical situation presents itself, you don't have to pause to wonder what you should do or stop to weigh the pros and cons, for you have already determined beforehand exactly how you should act. Your character is the result and compilation of all your life's choices up to date.

Character is more than just possessing intellect.

The true test of our character is not in what we know how to do, but in how we conduct ourselves when we don't exactly know what to do! Success, in most areas of life, depends more on character than on intellect. People do business with those they like and trust. Most people will continue to do business with people they may stop liking yet continue to trust. It doesn't matter how much people like another person—if they cannot trust that person, the chances of doing business are slim. If you have integrity and a strong, unwavering character, not much else matters. If you do not have integrity and an honorable character, to most people nothing else will make a difference.

Successful people in all walks of life have strong convictions and character and solid constitutions. They are overall very clear about who they are and what they stand for, what they will do, and what they won't do.

One question I have repeatedly pondered throughout my life is, why do we do what we do, when we supposedly know what we know? It all comes back to greatness or weakness of character. The odd thing about character is actions don't lie. True character is not how much we know or claim to know. And it is not what we do when we know what to do; rather, it is how we behave when we do not know what to do. Our true values and morals are revealed by what we do and how we handle the perceived crisis.

Learning to become a successful trader is all about having a *strong and solid character.* It is knowing what to do in a state of panic, in a state of a financial crisis, in a state when you think all may be potentially lost. When the market begins to race against you, when what started out to be a fun trading exercise has turned into a nightmare, the true you will come out. If you had any questions before on how to measure your character at trading, watch how you handle your trading crises and your actions will start to give you your answer.

Constitutionally Based and Feelings-Based People

Successful people live by what they believe, not by how they feel at the moment. People who live by what they believe are constitutionally based people, as compared to feelings-based people. Unsuccessful people are predominantly feelings-based rather than constitutionally based.

One of the main reasons our society is suffering from so many societal ills is due to weak character. In the last 50 years, our society has moved from being principle-based to being predominantly feelings-based. Millions of people today base most decisions on their feelings versus on their personal constitutions. Feelings-based people generally have difficulty solidifying plans, because if a better option comes along, they want to be free to do what they feel like doing. They don't go the extra mile, because it is too much work and they want to do as little as possible for as long as possible. They are more challenged in doing what is right than how they feel.

Quite the contrary, constitutionally based people do the right thing, whether it feels good or not, whether it is convenient or not, whether it is what they feel like doing or not, whether they have time to or not. They never pause to take a vote or get an opinion from their feelings before making a decision. They keep their priorities in check and are free from internal battles that create chaos, guilt, and weakness of character.

Feelings-based people generally walk around with high levels of guilt due to frequently ignoring their conscience and dulling the voice of reason. They often have low levels of self-esteem from underperformance at work. Perhaps they have been accused of being a bad friend, bad spouse, bad parent, bad employee, or bad family member. Their search for happiness to fill the self-inflicted voids in their life can lead them down a number of wrong roads.

Would you classify yourself as a feelings-based individual or a constitutionally based person? If you are a feelings-based person, you better not trade in any financial market, especially the Forex: the Forex will destroy you faster than your ability to get back on track.

> If you are a feelings-based person, you better not trade
> in any financial market, especially the Forex.

Your Character in Trading

Whatever your character consists of today, you will bring that to the trading table. If you are undisciplined in your personal life, you will be undisciplined at trading. If you are lazy in life, you will be lazy as you trade and will be constantly trying something new to try to get lucky. Whatever and whoever you are, as you look in the mirror, so will you be as you trade. If you think you will magically change and be someone different as you trade, then you are deceiving yourself.

So are you more of a feelings-based person or a constitutionally based one? How would you describe your personal character? Do you have a personal constitution? What are the rules and laws you live by? What rules and laws are you willing to easily break? Which ones are you not firm on? What are the rules and laws that are non-negotiable, that is, you will obey them in your day-to-day life? Take a moment to ask yourself if you are:

- A rule follower or a rule breaker?
- More honest, ethical, and fair, or more dishonest, unethical, and unfair?
- More selfish or unselfish?
- More disciplined, hardworking, driven, creative, positive? Or the opposite—self-indulgent, lazy, apathetic, unimaginative, and negative?

- High-achieving, energetic, strategic, organized, and proactive in everything you do? Or only in 50 percent of the things you do?
- Intuitive, objective, open-minded, optimistic, and teachable? Or more imperceptive, closed-minded, arrogant, and obtuse, walking around with a know-it-all attitude?
- Focused, intentional, and strategic about implementation when learning something new? Or easily distracted, scattered in thinking, impulsive, uncalculating, negligent, and careless, rendering you ineffective?
- Manage your emotions concerning financial risk, or mentally fall apart from the stress when things start to go wrong with your finances?
- Envision your success in the things you attempt to do, or carry an attitude of mediocrity, thinking, "I will never be super successful, I am just average"?

If you think your character will not have an effect on your trading outcome, you are grossly mistaken. The fact of the matter is your character has already had a given effect on your financial status and correlates with where you are currently in your life.

> If you think your character will not have an effect on
> your trading outcome, you are grossly mistaken.

No doubt there are things we cannot control in life such as where we were born, the class we were born into, predisposition, personality, physical appearance, and our capacity for knowledge, natural gifting, talent, and ability. These things play a big part in our current situations and circumstances. But success is about what we do with the things we can control, such as our education, personal growth and development, self-awareness, learned skills, and acquired knowledge. It is our life choices, actions, and behavior that create our character and ultimately our destiny.

A Trader's Constitution

As traders begin trading, they are learning disciplines of financial survival. They are learning the disciplines and skills of successful traders who trade for a living. What they are doing is slowly creating their trader's value system and code of ethics, which will define their actions; in other words, they are creating their trader's constitution. The process they go through is no different than the process we all go through from childhood to adulthood, growing up, experiencing life, and creating our own personal constitutions.

A trader's constitution is not a concept or document that restrains or limits a person's performance; rather, it safeguards and preserves a person's performance from being tarnished. It is a guideline created to allow freedom from financial harm as one trades. It becomes a person's compass to his or her destiny.

It is not wise to begin trading or to enter the market without a clear objective or purpose. I would not recommend entering the market with the aim of trying to get lucky, either. In reality, you cannot survive in the market with only luck. If you attempt to trade with a personal constitution called "lucky," it will only be a matter of time before the market renames your constitution as "unlucky." Learning to trade is a process, not a onetime event. There is no such thing as luck: either you are skilled or you are not skilled.

Defining your trading methodology, trader's rules, trader's value system, and trader's constitution will serve as a compass that will prevent you from straying off course. It will keep you from being tempted to enter the market when you shouldn't. Without a solid foundation, anything you try to build is destined to crumble and you will have to start all over again. Building a solid foundation, when it comes to trading, requires that you start knowing what you stand for and what you believe in.

We bring our character, our personal traits and habits, to the trading table. If we are undisciplined in our lives, we will be undisciplined at trading. If we don't go the extra mile in life, we won't go the extra mile when we trade. If we are unfocused in life, we will be unfocused as we trade. If we are looking to get lucky in life, we will look to get lucky as we trade.

> We bring our character, our personal traits
> and habits, to the trading table.

With absolutely no feeling, the market can drown you. Thousands of traders crash and burn each day, incurring irreparable damage because they let themselves get caught up in their fantasies of how the market would turn their financial world around. They strayed off course because they were unwilling to create a solid trading foundation: a sound trading strategy accompanied by a plan of action that they would be willing to obey. It is a sad day when you finally realize all the work you have done to date is reaping only trading injuries.

10 MAJOR BENEFITS OF WRITING A PERSONAL OR TRADER'S CONSTITUTION

1. **A constitution provides us with a purpose for what we are doing.** The reason we learn to trade is to make a profit. However, the greatest benefit I have received from learning to trade is how it completely changed many parts of my character and personality for the better.
2. **A constitution forces us to create a set of boundaries and rules for our safety.** Those rules create the boundaries of our performance and teach us to say no to the things that are not good for us and yes to the things that are good for us.
3. **A constitution helps us avoid mistakes in life that can result in bad consequences; this forces us to play closer attention to the rules.** Such situations cause us to be more disciplined, especially in trading when we make mistakes that have a negative financial consequence.

4. **A constitution helps us be disciplined to our beliefs, which gives us security and stability.** True stability takes place when there is ultimate order involved with the task at hand, and true order is when the presumed order is in balance with the disorder. A person then knows what to expect when the unexpected takes place.

5. **A constitution keeps us disciplined to our new rules.** When we incur a change of behavior and actions due to understanding a greater benefit in performing one way instead of another way, a huge benefit is our personality, reputation, and character change for the better.

6. **A constitution guides us and keeps us safe.** A clear constitution helps us understand ourselves better and provides us guidance for making decisions.

7. **A constitution becomes the policing force in our life.** It reminds us of our values and what is important to us when we are tempted to stray.

8. **Discipline to one's constitution reduces stress and can increase daily relaxation, especially as we trade.** You know your constitution is right when it tends to preserve the integrity and stability of all your relationships, especially the relationship you have with the market.

9. **A constitution eliminates a desire to blame.** Any successful person always accepts responsibility for what happens and focuses on fixing the problem instead of finding the blame.

10. **A constitution outlines our destiny as people and traders.** Destiny is not a matter of chance; it is a choice and decision we make. Our destiny changes with our thoughts and actions as we build a strong character.

Building Your Personal and Trader's Constitution

When creating a trader's constitution, you need to write down what you would like people to say about your work performance, especially in comparison to your knowledge of and education in your tasks at hand. What are they going to say about your work ethic and your true character at work? When it comes to creating your trader's constitution and a solid trading foundation, you need to be crystal clear on what you believe in, what you will do, what you won't do, and what you truly stand for. You need to have a deep understanding of your personal constitution—your personal moral constitution and the foundation that creates your reputation and character. Not only will you be replicating all those traits at the trading table, but they will become magnified as you execute trades.

Creating a constitution is basically simple and needs to be pure. A trader's constitution is determined through acquiring the proper knowledge about how the market works through trial and error as you learn the skills of trading, along with a persistent belief that in the end you will prevail as a successful trader; however, the foundation of your constitution will be laid by your character.

Creating a constitution is basically simple and needs to be pure.

FXCHIEF's PERSONAL CONSTITUTION

As an example, here is my personal trader's constitution:
I am a proficient, disciplined, and profitable Forex trader. I enjoy trading to make a profit. I honor the responsibility I have to myself and those who are watching and depending on me to be such a trader. Therefore:

- I continue to educate myself on how the market works.
- I know how to determine market direction, and I have a simple trading methodology that has an entry strategy and two exit strategies, one for profit and one for loss with equity management that feels comfortable to me and that I understand.

- I have a set of trading rules that make sense, and I obey my trading rules.
- I trade for pips and not for money.
- I trade nonemotionally. I turn off my profit-and-loss window on my dealing station to support this decision.
- I always trade with a protective stop-loss order.
- When I find a trade, I create a trading plan and trade my plan.
- If my currency of choice does not meet the criteria of my trading methodology, I look to trade another currency.
- If I cannot find a trade, I am patient and wait until the market meets the criteria of my trade.
- After each trade, I always win either pips or experience.

Our strong desire to become successful and excellent in everything we do is what gives us the courage to create a constitution that we begin to live by. A constitution that allows us to step up to the baseball plate of life and demand that we get to first base, then to second, and then third, until before we know it, we are consistently hitting home runs. Through persistence and discipline we can build our trader's constitution, lay the foundation of a successful trader's life, and learn how to execute all our trades correctly 100 percent of the time. Learning how to execute trades correctly is primarily based on three things:

- Learning market direction
- Having a solid entry strategy
- Having two clear exit strategies, one for profit and one to protect yourself should the market not go your way

These three simple steps are either taught through mentoring or figured out through trial and error with persistence. If you are trying to figure it out through trial and error, you not only better not run out of money from your mistakes, but you also better be true to your character, constitution, and disciplines until you to find the consistent trading strategy that works. If you are not a constitutionally based person, you will be constantly doing what feels good and trying different things. I call it "dropping the baby." Think about it: how many times can pediatricians, when delivering a child, afford to drop the baby? They can't, not even one time. It would be disastrous to their career. You cannot keep trying something new every other day based on your feelings of frustration. You must realize you cannot make money 100 percent of the time, but you can acquire the habit executing your trades 100 percent of the time according to your rules that work and become a winning trader, depositing ample money in your bank account even with a track record of only winning 50 percent of the time, provided you have the right equity management.

When it comes to trading, you get good by working hard; then you get better by practicing repetitiously a trading technique that you understand, is easy to obey, and fun to execute. Traders have a tendency to turn on their computers in the heat of battle and begin to execute trades with the utmost optimism, only to be disappointed when the trades turn out disastrous because the traders had no clear direction and wanted to feel the rush of winning by getting lucky. Then because they have no trader's constitution and trade based on only feelings, they search to place blame when they financially lose. They say, "What happened here? This is not my fault, I am much smarter than this! This system doesn't work, this market doesn't work, and this trading program doesn't work!"

Conclusion

Most of us pretty much know what we want out of life, what we want to become, what we want to do, and what we want to be. Yet we have a hard time getting there, because we don't know who we truly are and what we truly stand for. Worse yet, we don't know where to begin.

Creating your personal constitution will take time. It requires you to really look into the mirror and introspect. It requires you to compare yourself with other people who are more successful than you as well as those who are less successful than you. You will need to create a careful self-analysis, constantly asking yourself what you really want out of life and what quality of life you want or realistically expect to achieve.

In the end, you need to feel comfortable with your final draft of your constitution, believing you can live by what you are writing. It needs to be the ultimate expression of your innermost values and beliefs that will stand as your compass in life, giving you direction to your desired destiny. As time passes by, you will gain greater experience in life and your circumstances will change. When they do, you will want to revisit your constitution and even update it with minor changes in the spirit of improving the quality of your life. Your constitution will be your clear vision of how you want your world to be and will reveal to the world who you truly are.

CHAPTER 9

DEALING WITH FRUSTRATION AS YOU TRADE

Most of our behavior is driven by our feelings. Where is your gauge for finding and maintaining happiness? Happiness is not simply the absence of despair; it is an affirmative state in which our lives have both meaning and purpose while experiencing pleasure. Every one of us needs to look at the way we are living, because if we are not clear on our purpose and direction, we will begin to experience spurts of frustration that turn into overall days of frustration and ultimately a life of frustration.

As most of us finally discover, neither money nor the lack of it are assurances of happiness. It is not having what you want that leads to happiness, but rather wanting what you have. An emotionally secure and tranquil mind is a happy mind. The more you are willing to learn what is right, what works, how to help people, give more than you take, and to be who you are and what you are, the more certain you can be that happiness will find you. Just as with success, you cannot find happiness—it must find you.

Happiness, therefore, is the consequences of our mindset and attitudes. To be happy, you must walk around with a happy attitude and live a happy life. You must be like the boy who upon entering a room full of horse manure gets super excited and starts jumping for joy, smiling and saying, "With this much horse manure, there must be a pony in here somewhere!"

> Happiness is the consequences of
> our mindset and attitudes.

After you get started trading, if things don't go according to plan, you are going to feel you have entered into a room full of horse manure. What you do with your attitude at that moment will determine your overall outcome. The best emotional state to live and trade in is a happy one, and a mindset of happiness is a great ingredient for success. There are three key components for creating happiness in our life: doing something that we really enjoy, finding someone to love and share our life experiences with, and having something to look forward to.

Your Frustration with the Market and Trading

If you are already trading in the market, and if you find yourself frequently thinking of the word *frustration*, do some of the following thoughts come to mind?

- "I don't have a clear strategy."
- "I don't know what I am doing."
- "These markets are impossible."
- "I'm a loser, a fool, an idiot."
- "I'll never get the hang of this."
- "I'm too small, inexperienced, young, old, . . ."
- "What will X think of me? I told him this works."
- "The market is rigged."
- "I can't get a decent fill."
- "My broker is out to get me."
- "This game is impossible to win."
- "If I take a loss, then I am a loser."
- "I will never have a winning trade."

The first few years of my trading career were frustrating beyond explanation. Before I figured out how to properly deal with my frustrations, I was always looking for someone to blame. I did not have a mentor. I did not have anyone to answer my questions. The charting software I used didn't even have the necessary indicators, such as the Fibonacci tools I needed to become successful. All I saw on a daily basis was chaos in the market with no rhyme or reason as to why it did what it did.

My frustration and emotions were controlling my universe and taking me down a path of self-destruction. It now reminds me of the joke about the difference between a hurricane and the market: What do hurricanes and the market have in common? They both sweep you off your feet when they come into your life, and when they leave, they both take everything you have.

As I progressed in my trading career, I always found some other obstacle in the way, something I had to figure out, something I had to work through first, some emotion I had to conquer, some unfinished business somewhere. I would say, "As soon as I overcome this, my true trader's life will begin." At last, it dawned on me that those obstacles were a major part of my life, and to find success I would need to change several aspects of my personal life, especially managing my levels of frustration.

The torment and frustration I went through to discover all this was equal to being locked in prison with a mangled mind filled with wasteful self-conflict. What would happen to me is when I chose to discuss my frustrations with others, I started to see a pattern in the people whom I talked with—80 percent didn't care what I was going through and the other 20 percent were glad to see me frustrated and suffering. Very few were willing to help.

You are the only one making the decision about where to get in the market and where to get out. If you are not incurring the financial success you are looking for, you, and you alone, are to blame. Of course frustration will follow. However, it is how you deal with that frustration that will determine your performance at the trading table.

Staying Focused

Watch what can happen when traders step back from their negative emotions and frustrations and stay focused on the task at hand. Look at everything I have discovered and put together by doing so:

- The A, B, C, D price movement of the rally, retracement, and extension relationships
- Looking for and using three trend lines versus using just one
- Trading the harmonic beats
- How to trade the Fibonacci numbers and their relationship with their extensions
- The five steps to the King's crown (which came to me after I lost so much money and out of my frustrations with trading the head-and-shoulders pattern)

I have come to believe that all my past failures and frustrations were actually helping me become a better person, become a better trader, and lay the foundation for the discovery of all the information I am sharing with you.

I also discovered that my frustrations were standing in the way of my ability to think and figure things out. That discovery has enhanced many facets of my personal life. The challenge was to discover how to deal with my frustrations at trading and how to turn feelings of frustration into productive plans of action for successful trading.

The wager with the highest stakes, in my opinion, is what we do with our emotions as we feel our way through life and trading. Where do we learn how to handle our emotions as we learn to trade? How do we balance the risk in trading, knowing that at the end of the trade we will either win or lose, and knowing that if we make a mistake and lose money, it will create emotional pain and be a financial burden? Unlike most games, the outcome in this one is meant to dramatically reward the winner and will certainly destroy the loser, emotionally as well as financially. In the game of trading, the person who masters his or her emotions and frustration wins.

In the game of trading, the person who masters
his or her emotions and frustration wins.

It has been said that life is a game, and the person who dies
with the most toys wins. Well, we all know that isn't necessarily
true, but everyone who is attempting to make money trading really
wants deep inside to use that money to either enhance their life or
ease their burden in this life. Is making money at whatever cost the
game you want to play with your life? Is that what you want your
loved ones to say at your funeral? "Well, he did have the most toys,
so the winner is . . ." When you pass on, what do you want said
about the person you were? What kind of legacy do you want to
leave behind?

Traders who fail to achieve their goals usually get stopped by
a lack of discipline and loss of focus, allowing their emotions and
frustrations to rule their actions. The only way to get through this
roadblock is by understanding what causes frustration and then
plowing through it.

What do you do when you get frustrated?

What creates frustrations? It is having expectations. When you
create any expectation in any part of your life, you have taken the
first step to inviting frustration into your life. If there is no expectation, there can be no frustration. Frustration only exists when an
expectation is set. If an expectation is set and not met, frustration
will appear, knock at the front door of your emotions, and demand
to be let in. It usually is accompanied with its close friends: anger,
anxiety, depression, despair, madness, insanity, confusion, finding fault, and wanting to blame. Once you allow frustration and
its friends to occupy your mind, your emotions and performance
become temporarily derailed.

Of course, we must have expectations. In all fairness, we know
we cannot live a life without expectations. However, many times
we fall short when we create unrealistic or greater-than-necessary
expectations for the situation than we ought to. We set ourselves
up for emotional failure and invite the frustration in.

FRUSTRATION QUIZ

Answer the following five questions:

1. When a situation does not meet your expectations and you become frustrated, do you immediately look to place blame first by asking, "Who did this?"

    _____ Yes

    _____ No

2. If the situation frustrates you emotionally, is your habit to emotionally react or mentally respond?_____

3. If the situation frustrates you emotionally, do you speak first before you think or do you think through the situation well before you speak?_____

4. If the situation frustrates you emotionally, do you feel better venting and alleviating your dissatisfaction, or do you feel better thinking and setting up guidelines, rules, and disciplines to avoid that situation again? _____

5. After an average daily situation that frustrates you is over, how much time do you waste thinking about it or fretting over it?

    _____ 2–5 minutes

    _____ 5–30 minutes

    _____ 30 minutes to several hours

    _____ the rest of the day

If you answered the preceding questions in the following ways, then you have formed an unhealthy habit in dealing with your daily frustrations.

1. Yes, I have a need to blame.

2. Yes, I emotionally react.

3. Yes, I speak before I think.

4. Yes, I prefer venting and alleviating my stress first before acting.

5. Yes, I take much longer than 5 minutes to get over frustrating situations.

You will bring these bad habits to the trading table, and they will stand in the way of your trading success.

Mismanaged frustrations when trading will only cause you to stay focused on sending out invitations to your own pity party rather than on figuring out how the market works and how to jump in and take advantage of it. Uncontrolled frustration will cause you to agonize instead of organize. Unrestrained frustration will stump your trading progress.

Mismanaged frustrations will cause you to stay focused on sending out invitations to your own pity party.

I know the price a trader must pay for success. It's hidden under the words *dedication, hard work, hope, trust, conviction, believing, confidence,* and *self-respect.* Success is a relentless devotion to your belief that the things you are working on will happen. All successful traders learn that frustration is buried on the other side of success. Staying focused and learning to master your frustrations in trading is an important part of a trader's armor and is vital to his or her success.

Indifference

Although quite painful at times, frustration can be a very positive and essential part of your trading success. Putting your frustration into perspective and maintaining a positive attitude will override your negative thought processes and balance out how far you have come with how far you need to go.

All that is needed to break the spell of frustration in your trading career is to replace that feeling of frustration with the feeling of indifference. Indifference safeguards you. Feeling indifferent is placing yourself in a position where you will not take things personally; therefore, your mind does not activate the feelings of frustration and shut off access to the left side of your brain, which is where all your recall is regarding how to successfully trade.

The definition of indifference is the absence of anxiety or inter-est in respect to what is presented to the mind: unconcerned, hav-ing no feeling toward all that occurs. Indifference as you trade is one of the first steps to figuring out a trading methodology that works. Frustration prevents you from figuring things out, while learning the skill of how to be indifferent about the potential nega-tive things that will happen to you will keep you focused on prob-lem solving and creating a trading methodology that coincides or agrees with your personality.

When applied at trading, indifference is the strongest force in the universe. It makes everything it touches meaningless. If you can acquire indifference as you trade, you will learn to trade with no emotion. Love and hate are emotions. Love is a powerful emo-tion. Hate is a stronger emotion. What is the opposite of love? Most people say hate. It is not hate. As long as there is hate, there is emotion and the potential for that hate to turn around and become love. The opposite of love is indifference, not hate. Indifference is to not feel either way. It is a mindset of just doing what needs to be done without feeling. In other words, you are trying to learn how to trade as a robot, making decisions based on the given tried-and-true formulas and not on a whim of a rogue emotion.

Love and hate don't stand a chance against indifference. We don't want to take the emotions of love and hate out of our daily lives. But we do want to take emotions out of trading. Indifference in trading is then a learned and disciplined skill that needs to be turned into a mindset. It participates in your formula for trading success.

When you turn on your computer to trade, you are there to execute a task. Your goal as a successful trader is to capture pips. You believe your goal is to make money. Well, the reality is that you need to make money; however, being a successful trader is like being a successful doctor. Doctors as a rule do not focus on making money. They have educated themselves to understand the patients' signs and symptoms and then provide them with a health plan for recovery—all this without feeling. They don't emotionally get involved with their patients. A standing rule for doctors is they cannot operate on a family member, because of the emotional tie to the patient. They need to keep their distance from their patients, avoiding any emotion and exacting all precision. Trading must be the same.

As a trader, you cannot afford to get emotionally involved with the market. It will only cause you frustration. You cannot trade for money and be successful. Trading for money is not the key to successful trading. The key to successful trading is found when you take the focus off the money and put all your focus on the skill and proficiency of executing a trading plan that makes sense according to your education, just like the doctor does.

Learning how to be indifferent as you trade is the first step to understanding that your subconscious mind will close the door to the right side of the brain where your emotion is found and open the door to the left side of your brain where all your recall is in relation to all the things you have learned and all the things you need to implement to become a good trader.

Six-Step Process to Becoming Indifferent

I have created a process that will help you become indifferent as you trade by doing the following:

1. Write down what your expectations are at trading. Now dramatically lower them. If one is to make 500 pips a month trading, lower it to 50 pips a month. If it is to be correct 90 percent of the time, lower it to 30 percent of the time. Right now, lower your expectations about your desired results.
2. Figure out and write down all the things that frustrate you presently as you trade. Is it losing money, getting stopped out, being wrong, or not finding a trade when it's time to trade?
3. Mentally walk through what you are going to do when an expectation is not met. Are you going to scream and yell looking for someone to blame? Are you going to control your

emotions or let your emotions control you? Are you going to act before you think or think before you act?

4. Face your worst fear in trading. What is the worst thing that can happen to you? Keep in mind, the market can only take what you allow it to with your predetermined stop loss. You are in control.

5. Put the worst thing that can happen to you into perspective. Compared to what? Think forward to your next trade, think through what will happen if you lose on your next trade, and put it into perspective.

6. Buy into the rule that nothing in trading can be emotional. This must become a rule. You cannot feel as you trade. You cannot attach your ego or self-worth to the trade. You are either a winner emotionally before you trade or you are not.

Walking through these steps may make the difference between the trader you want to be and what you are willing to sacrifice to become that trader.

Reaching a Turning Point

You will reach your turning point as a trader the moment you stop getting frustrated about not making the money you want at trading and start working on mastering the art of trading via your disciplines, skills, and trading methodologies.

Life is about effective problem solving. Every day when I get up, I prepare myself to solve problems. As a matter of fact, I consider myself to be a very effective problem solver. I used to answer yes to the five questions in the earlier quiz, but today I must admit that for the 95 percent of my life that is used in problem solving, I now answer no to those five questions.

Life is about effective problem solving.

There is no way people can be successful in life if they are constantly frustrated. Nor can they really have a fighting chance at success if they are not effective problem solvers. Have you ever watched very successful people solve a problem? They are usually methodical and unemotional. For them, problems are all nothing more than a mathematical equation: $2 + 2 = 4$, period. Have you ever watched an out-of-control person try to solve a problem?

Learning the new skill of controlling your frustration so that it does not control you can change your life forever. We are talking about purging your bad habit of ineffective problem solving and reprogramming your thinking to implement new personal restraints, enabling you to become a better problem solver, a better person, and a better trader as you handle your daily frustrations in life and in trading.

Acceptance of responsibility for how we feel, what we do, and what we say as we work through problems is a major step in dealing with frustration. We have no say over the emotions that surface and how we feel when presented with a problem. We do, however, have a say over how we respond to that problem.

Positive Versus Negative Thinking

Most of the time we don't see things as *they* are, we see things as *we* are. If we are optimists, we see things in an optimistic manner; if we gravitate toward being pessimist, we see things in a pessimistic manner.

In dealing with our trading frustrations, we must maintain the outlook of a positive-thinking optimist. When first trading, most people become excited and are positive about its potential, but after about three months, the honeymoon is over and their true personality comes out. They either dig in and become more positive, or they start to buy into their beliefs that it is much too hard. They turn more negative, and that is how they will move forward in their learning curve.

Open-minded traders excel at a greater rate than closed-minded traders. It is hard for the human person to learn in a state of frustration. Frustration multiplies. It creates additional frustrations and challenges for the trader. A stumbling block to the pessimist is a stepping stone to the optimist.

> Open-minded traders excel at a greater
> rate than closed-minded traders.

Look at all the great things in life accomplished by people with positive attitudes—people willing to plow through frustration and whatever obstacle that stands in their way. How many things in life have been accomplished with a positive attitude versus a negative one? We must move forward believing and expecting the very best to start getting the very best, even if it is not the very best at the time.

If you are not making the money in your life that you always dreamed of, perhaps it is because you are locked into a series of unproductive work habits and destructive mindsets. Perhaps you have created a mental block inside you that has stopped you from earning more than you think you are worth. If you want to earn more than you are earning right now, you must upgrade your self-concept and self-worth.

Concentrate on the positive: think positive, look for positive, and act positive. Where you see the positive, you call forth more positive. Where you see the negative, you call forth more negative. It is the application of the law of focus and concentration, similar to the law of attraction.

Conclusion

No situation is so hard or bad that you can't make it easier by the way you absorb it, view it, think about it, process it, and respond to it. The eye can see only what the mind is prepared to comprehend.

As we think about situations dealing with frustration, we draw on all our past positive and negative experiences that have shaped our lives and formulated our predisposed opinions. If we have experienced great pain and sorrow, we move forward in life with extreme caution in hopes of avoiding more sorrow and pain.

What you think, see, and hear depends a good deal on what you have experienced in life and where you are at the moment you need to start to form that perception. A large part of creating a perception of reality also depends on what sort of person you are. If you are more of a pessimist than an optimist and are always distressed and frustrated about things, the reality you will create for yourself will be more negative than positive.

As you learn how to trade, you must keep your perception of what is going on in check. Once again, we don't see things as *they* are, we see them as *we* are. If we approach trading as winners, we will probably win more than lose. If we approach trading with frustration and insecurity encompassing a losing attitude, we will lose more than we will win. What the caterpillar calls the end of its life, the rest of the world, along with the butterfly, calls a birth or a new beginning. Every exit is an entry to somewhere. And oftentimes it is only afterward that we realize it was a blessing in disguise.

CHAPTER 10

DEALING WITH ANGER AS YOU TRADE

If you do not wish to be prone to anger, do not feed the habit; give it nothing that will make it grow stronger. Anger is an emotional state that varies in intensity from mild irritation to intense fury and rage, depending on the potential perceived threat. Anger is ultimately a form of fear. When we feel any threat to our life or to our comfortable state of mind, we start to incur physiological and biological changes. When we get angry, our heart rate, blood pressure, energy, hormones, adrenaline, and noradrenalin go up. Our bodies begin to experience biological changes and enter into a small state of metamorphosis.

Anger can be caused by both external and internal events. You could be angry at a specific person who you feel has offended you or at an event like someone pulling out in front of you in traffic. Your anger could also be caused from within, by worrying or stewing about your personal problems, feeling overwhelmed with your work load at your job or responsibilities in the home, feeling inadequate, or having no self-esteem. Traumas from our past or events that we recall also trigger feelings of anger.

When you get upset, mad, or angry about anything in life, how long do you feed that anger before you can emotionally move on? A few minutes? An hour? Half a day? The entire rest of the day?

No doubt, our objective in life is to be happy and productive. Thousands of books have been written on finding the formula for happiness. For 30 years I looked for happiness, thinking that if I had more money, a nicer car, lived in a bigger house or a nicer neighborhood, had nicer furniture, or could travel and experience more exotic vacations, I would be happier. After those 30 years, however, I never found happiness; it was always fleeting with each new thing I acquired. I now needed to *live* my happiness and live it on a daily basis.

For every minute you remain angry, you give up 60 seconds of happiness. Human beings were created to wake up every morning and be happy. Learning the skills of emptying yourself of anger on a daily basis will change your life dramatically. It is one of the key skills one must learn to achieve success at anything.

> For every minute you remain angry, you
> give up 60 seconds of happiness.

You must realize that this life is not fair and bad things will happen to everyone, including you. You will be blindsided from time to time as you learn to trade on the Forex. You will be ecstatic in the beginning because you will feel you just found a mountain of gold, and in fact you did. Your challenge will be learning the physical and emotional skill to extract that gold.

Success does not find those who get mad, angry, and disappointed, allowing resentment to build and if left to fester, take root to bitterness. It is a tragic thing when we let the disappointments in life scar us so badly that we become immobilized by a victim mentality.

Get on Track to Productivity

Your success or failure in Forex trading will be determined by what you do when you experience problems or run into obstacles in the market. You will have to make choices along the way, and the choices you make will determine the quality and outcome of your experience. You will need to decide between:

- Disappointment or reappointment
- Resentment or resilience
- Bitter or better
- Whiner or winner
- Crumbler or conqueror
- Victim or victor
- Living with a scar or turning it into a star

Your decisions will determine your Forex experience and your quality of life.

Life is about waking up every day with purpose and loving what we do. When we incur an event that makes us angry, we take our focus off of achieving the task at hand and focus on working through our uninvited negative emotions. The longer we linger working through this anger, the less productive we are. It is not that working through our negative emotions is counterproductive or of no value. Rather, if we learn to effectively and efficiently work through our negative emotions, we will enable ourselves to stay focused on the original task at hand. Clearly, it is unhealthy to pretend negative emotions do not exist. Working through them is good and healthy. We must take some time to examine, sift, and work through them before we can make the choice to purge them and replace them with the proper, positive, helpful emotions we need. This whole process is necessary for us to get back on track toward being productive.

When anger appears in our lives and is not immediately dealt with, it becomes cancerlike. Once contracted, it spreads, and if undetected, it will corrode our personality and eat away at our inner being. Anger is all-consuming and does not restrain from damaging our soul and tainting our life. You may have heard the caution "Don't let the sun go down on your anger." There is something unseen and powerful about harboring anger in your heart and letting it reside there. In a state of anger, people destroy their sense of values and lose sight of their objectivity.

Anger causes people to describe the beautiful as ugly and the ugly as beautiful, and to confuse the truth with what is false and the false with what is true. In the end, anger is an acid that can do more harm inside a person where it is stored than to any surface it is poured on. Anger is all-consuming and numbs logic and sensibility. The instant we feel anger and decide to entertain it is the moment we begin to impact our quality of life, as there is no stability in anger. Anger makes us smaller people.

Our anger always comes from expectations that have not been met. Those unmet expectations start off with frustration, creating bitterness and leading to anger. Feelings of anger are a normal by-product of certain events and situations and are a part of everyone's life, but when not properly dealt with, anger turns completely self-destructive, especially for traders in the market.

If you are currently trading, how often do you get angry during a trade or after a trade? How many times in a day does this anger surface over trades that did not go your way? After you have lost on a trade, how often do you feel upset or mad or act outright spiteful to other people you come into contact with? People who don't know how to control their anger and fly into rages always make bad landings. I have learned that whatever angers you controls you. Anger is a terrible counselor or mentor in the market.

Anger is a terrible counselor or mentor in the market.

Experiencing Anger in Life and Trading

Anger is perceived to be an unhealthy emotion, but in reality it is usually a healthy human emotion that helps us process information about events in our lives. It becomes unhealthy when it gets out of control and turns ugly or destructive. Our emotions help the weight or gravity of a certain situation be driven home. They are a guide as to what is important to us.

Emotions can be a clear indicator as to what is going on inside us. And it is worthwhile to take a good look inside when our emotions start rising with intensity, whatever they may be. The healthy way to process any emotion is to begin by acknowledging it and saying to yourself, "I feel this emotion coming on strong." Then analyze it for any truth or validity. Locate its source and find what is causing it. Troubleshoot the potential problem or situation for a healthy resolution. Make a conscious effort to exhale anger and inhale indifference so that you can think clearly. And focus your energy on the plan of action and achieving closure.

I realize that this is often easier said than done; however, remember that practice makes habit! Do this several times, and you will be well on your way to mastering the habit of emotional intelligence.

People who are unable to manage their anger usually create additional problems for themselves that can lead to problems at work, in trading, in personal relationships, and in the overall quality of their daily life. Out-of-control anger can make you feel as though you're at the mercy of a powerful emotion, which can create unpredictable, damaging actions.

Anger is a very strong emotion that can create a lot of damage to yourself and others if not properly channeled. Things said in anger can sting, offend, destroy relationships, and even start wars. Unfortunately, we cannot reverse time and undo the damage created by the angry words spoken. When we give the angry virus the approval to spread and grow inside us, we begin to self-destruct. With anger in control, we enter into an unconscious state of fear and now begin focusing on self-preservation.

When anger surfaces, and we incur an emotional hijacking for the moment, reacting and exploding, after everything is said and done (and usually more is always said than ever done), we realize that the issue really didn't matter. A helpful way I have learned to deal with my anger when it surfaces is to take a deep breath and ask myself the following before I react or explode on someone else:

Will this matter next week?
Will this matter next month?
Will this matter next year?

Using this method can help you gain perspective on the gravity of the issue that is angering you or that is creating your tumultuous emotions. Most people never take the time to realize that their anger hurts them more than anyone else. When you get mad or angry about something—such as a trade that did not go your way and did not work out—many times you incur an emotional hijacking and enter into a tailspin of emotional destruction. After you land and assess the damage, you usually find that more hurt has been done to you than anyone else.

People who are easily angered generally have a low tolerance for frustration. They mostly think they are better than others, and they feel they should not have to be subjected to any frustration, inconvenience, or annoyance. It is very difficult for them to deal with issues they perceive as unjust, and they become particularly infuriated from being corrected for minor mistakes.

What makes these people this way? Research has shown that a number of things play a big role with anger issues, especially family background. People who are easily angered usually come from families that are disruptive and chaotic, contain high stress levels, are aggressive in their communications, have limited skills for communicating, and have virtually no emotional intelligence. Additionally, anger may be genetic, physiological, or due to a chemical imbalance. There is evidence that some children from birth are irritable, sensitive, and easily angered, and signs of this become prevalent in early childhood. It is a fact that some people are really more hotheaded and have more anger-management challenges than others.

For most parents, anger is often considered negative. People are taught that it is all right to express anxiety, depression, or other emotions, but it is not acceptable behavior to express anger. As a result of that mindset, people are not taught how to deal with anger and don't learn how to handle it or channel it constructively.

Handling Anger

There are three predominant ways that the majority of people handle their anger: expressing, suppressing, and calming down.

Most people express their angry feelings in an unproductive unhealthy way by throwing a temper tantrum, screaming, yelling, and blaming others. Angry people tend to curse, swear, or speak in highly colorful terms that reflect their inner thoughts. When you're angry, your thinking can become exaggerated and overly dramatic. I have seen countless traders throw their computers, kick their desks, kick their dog, and scream and yell every obscenity in the book.

The healthiest way to handle anger if you feel the need to outwardly express it is to apply emotional intelligence (remember the lessons from Chapter 6). Think before responding, and after you have thought through a productive solution, be assertive, not aggressive; be calm and concise in your communications; and make clear what your needs are with your solution and how to meet them without hurting others. You have to learn how to be assertive, not pushy or demanding; it means being respectful to yourself and others during the process. No doubt, it takes practice to become emotionally intelligent while controlling your anger.

It takes practice to become emotionally
intelligent while controlling your anger.

The second way to deal with anger is to suppress it. Anger is not only displayed in lashing out, but can be displayed by being chronically irritable or grumpy. Easily angered people don't always curse, throw things, or get physical; sometimes they withdraw socially or begin to sulk privately. There are also two ways of suppressing your anger; one is healthy and one is unhealthy.

The healthy way is to convert your anger into useful information and then constructively work that information to your advantage. The real aim is not to suppress your anger, but to quietly convert it into a more constructive behavior by focusing on positive thinking and positive solutions.

The unhealthy way of suppressing your anger is to stop thinking about it completely, to sweep it under the rug, ignore it, and pretend you feel nothing. The danger in this type of response is that if the anger isn't allowed some sort of expression, your anger can turn inward and make you feel miserable. Because you have suppressed the anger, you may not always be aware of why you feel miserable. This is dangerous and is an emotional dead end. Or you can compare it to a pinched water line; it is only a matter of time before it will blow. Anger turned inward may cause hypertension, high blood pressure, or depression.

Unhealthy suppressed anger can create other external problems for ourselves. It can lead to pathological expressions of anger, such as passive-aggressive behavior. Suppressed anger can also create a cynical and hostile personality. People who are constantly putting others down, criticizing everything, and making cynical comments haven't learned how to constructively express their anger. It is very difficult for cynical people to have many successful relationships.

Finally, the calming-down approach is where you take a deep breath, step back, and calm down inside. This means not just controlling your outward behavior, but also controlling your internal responses, like taking steps to lower your heart rate, breathe deeply to calm yourself down, and allow the feelings to subside. It's best to find out what it is that triggers your anger and then have some developed strategies ready to keep those triggers from tipping you over the edge. Consider the following techniques to help you calm down:

1. Excuse yourself from the situation and go for a walk or sit alone in a room where you can think without interruption.
2. Breathe deeply from your diaphragm and not from your chest, as breathing from your chest won't relax you. Picture your breath coming up from your stomach.
3. Slowly repeat a calm word or phrase such as "just relax," "take it easy," or "this, too, will pass," while breathing deeply.
4. Visualize a relaxing experience, like sitting under a waterfall, staring at a fire, or looking at the ocean.
5. Count to 10 before you speak. If very angry, count to 100.
6. Excuse yourself to go and exercise, and work out your anger or frustrations, if the situation does not warrant an immediate response. Perhaps you can get involved with nonstrenuous, calming yoga. Try to exercise and relax your muscles, which can make you feel much calmer as exercise releases endorphins and mood elevation is a natural by-product. Endorphins flowing and blood pumping also cause your mind to think clearer and be sharper.

Recognizing that anger is a part of our lives and implementing ways to deal with it are both healthy and productive. Living in denial and not recognizing that anger can enter our lives at any time on a daily basis can ultimately alter the quality of life we are entitled to.

Those people involved in out-of-control anger are ones who manage their poverty or mediocrity. It is not a habit of the successful. The real reality is that angry people are people who are the most afraid. Think about it!

Trading Better Through Controlling Your Anger

Decision making in a state of anger is never wise. When trading, do you know why you get mad, frustrated, or angry? When you trade and get mad, do you know the root cause? Is it because of any of the following:

- Creating false or unmet expectations?
- Trading without really knowing what you are doing?
- Living in denial about your ability?
- Feeling desperate about not knowing how to make up your losses? (After all, if you properly knew how to trade and make up all your losses, you would never get mad.)
- Not finding productive trades that make money in the time slot you have to trade?

I really believe the art of successful living is closely tied to being able to manage and control your anger, and the art of successful trading is the ability to master your anger, enabling you to master the market. Success at trading is closely tied to our ability to harness our negative emotions. When we are full of anger, we think on anger's terms.

The art of successful trading is the ability to master your anger.

How many times have you flown off the handle without knowing all the facts? How many times were you quick to accuse in a state of anger before you gathered all the facts? Holding your tongue, avoiding confrontation, and taking the high road can be hard, but they are also necessary.

No one is perfect. I think it's fair to say we have all made mistakes we are not proud of. The beautiful thing about life is second chances. Every morning we wake up is a second chance to redo our yesterday and learn from our mistakes and move on. It is of no value to look back at situations that angered us or to look forward with fear. There is a reason the windshield is 100 times larger and clearer than the rearview mirror. It is our responsibility to learn from our mistakes, learn from the negative experiences that angered us, and take the time to educate ourselves about the things in life we are involved in so we can look around with awareness. Emotional intelligence and learning to manage our anger is the ability to listen to almost anything without losing your temper, your self-confidence, or your self-esteem. When you make wrong decisions at trading, you are going to get mad, even angry. Whatever you do, stop to learn from the lesson so you can avoid the situation in the future. If you don't take the time to dissect and evaluate what made you angry, you are prone to repeat it over and over in your life.

Remind yourself that the worst time to try to problem solve is when in a state of anger. Getting angry is not going to fix anything, it is not going to make you feel better, and as a matter of fact, your anger may actually make you feel worse. Calming down and opening up the tube that leads to your left brain and inviting logic to appear while you are in a state of anger is the answer to suppressing the anger. Logic defeats anger and is the antidote to getting rid of it. Look at things logically, and realize that angry people tend to demand the same things we want: respect, fairness, appreciation, recognition, equitable agreement, a willingness to do things their way. We all want these things, and we are hurt and disappointed when we don't get them. But angry people demand them, and when their demands aren't met, their disappointment turns into anger.

> The worst time to try to problem solve is when in a state of anger.

The goal in learning to manage your anger is to learn how to reduce both your emotional feelings and the physiological arousal over those things that anger you. You can't get rid of or even avoid the things or people who enrage you, nor can you change them. But you can learn to control your reactions. To be able to put your anger into proper perspective and be angry with the right person over the right thing, to the right degree, at the right time, for the right purpose, and in the right way is not easy.

The bigger question is when anger appears inside you, what are you going to do about it? How are you going to process it or deal with it to where the outcome is productive and toward your benefit?

Buddha said, "Holding on to anger is like grasping a hot coal with the intent of throwing it on someone else; you are the one who gets burned." Holding onto anger, resentment, or any kind of hurt can only give you tense muscles, headaches, chest pain, stomach ulcers, and a sore jaw from clenching your teeth. Anger will never disappear so long as thoughts of hatred or resentment are cherished in the mind. Forgiveness is the key that gives you back your laughter, happiness, and a focused direction. Our happiness in life is closely tied to our ability to forgive. If you can't forgive, and I mean totally forgive, you will struggle with getting rid of anger and you will struggle with your happiness. Every time you think about that situation, person, or event, your feelings will go right back to that point in time and force you to relive the event while the happy feelings you were experiencing change. You will now resurrect the dead and relive that emotional experience.

Forgiveness, believe it or not, is not for the weak. Forgiveness is only for the strong. When people make mistakes, even loved ones, forgive them. It is your key to happiness. I was in Toronto teaching a class of advanced traders when I asked them what issues they were still working on as traders. To my surprise, one trader said he had been trading for four years and was still struggling with forgiving himself when he makes mistakes. I thought to myself, forgiveness is the key to moving on. Forgive yourself and move forward!

Conclusion

The focus of successful traders is no different than that of professional tennis players. Professional tennis players don't worry about or waste time thinking about the ball they just missed or the point they just lost. Nor do they worry or even think about the next set. Their sole focus is to purge themselves of any and all negative feelings or thoughts and place themselves in a winning mental position to successfully hit the next ball coming and to focus only on the next ball coming. Players know that the next ball is the one that counts and they cannot afford to waste any negative emotional energy or time on the ball just missed. At the same time they don't want to waste any emotion or energy on how things could have been or how things will be if they win in the end. They care only about putting their head, heart, positive emotions, and skills all in place to successfully hit the next ball.

Retrospect is good, but it should be saved for later reflection and only for the purpose of training and education so you don't repeat the same mistake. The past is not to be dredged up with all kinds of shame and feelings of disappointment, rehearsing our failure. As the saying goes, appropriate recall needs to be saved for after the game in the locker room; it is to be replayed with the intent of analyzing mistakes and recapped with a new game plan. A Forex trader needs to do the same. It doesn't matter what happened in the last trade; it's over and it's time to move on. Blessed is he who doesn't show anger or hatefulness over what is lost but instead shows gratefulness for what is left!

CHAPTER 11

ALTER YOUR ATTITUDE, ALTER YOUR TRADING RESULTS

Every great achievement started with a thought; then that thought turned into a belief. Then that belief turned into a series of actions, and little by little over time, those actions achieved the original dream. Look back at anything you have achieved. Your first bicycle, your first car, your first house, your first job, your first partner, and the list goes on. They all began with an original thought about a dream you wanted to come true, and with the right concentration and focus they slowly became a reality. In other words, you map out your future and your thoughts, and you have the power to eventually become your own fortune-teller, your own personal prophesier. First the thought, then the action! Since you are reading this book, you have already been introduced to the Forex and you are wondering if it could be your new path to financial success. Hope is the faith that leads to achievement. Nothing can be achieved without hope. Successful trading on the Forex is not a fantasy, it's a formula, and a critical ingredient to that formula is attitude.

More than anything else, our attitude at the beginning of any challenging or difficult task will affect the outcome. A positive attitude is the high-performance fuel that keeps the engine running. Without that fuel, no one goes anywhere. Having a positive mental attitude is similar to having a GPS in your car: you never get lost because you have the excitement and optimism that you can achieve anything and that gives you the courage to never give up.

Rather than caving into your negative attitude and saying, "It can't be done," you never stop asking how something must get done.

A positive mental attitude keeps your mind optimistic rather than pessimistic, helping you believe that nothing is impossible. Everything is solvable, and there is nothing that cannot be achieved. Sometimes we are more limited by our attitude than we are by opportunities, and more often than not, the only disability we walk around with is our bad attitude.

The amazing thing about life is that we wake up every morning with the freedom to choose whether to have a great attitude or a bad attitude. Picture choosing your attitude for the day, just as you pick out the clothes you will wear. The choice we make determines the outcome of our day, and the outcome of our days determines the outcome of our weeks, and the outcome of our weeks determine the outcome of our months, which determines our years, which determines our lives.

The longer I live, the more I realize how important attitude is and the impact it has on the human life. Attitude is more important than education. I would rather work with an uneducated optimist than I would with an educated pessimist. How about you? Attitude is more important than looks, money, skill or talent, material things, or being born into royalty. It is more important than what people think, say, or do. Attitude will make or break a dream, a project, or a great company, and even tear apart our most treasured possessions in life: our relationships with loved ones and family. It will wreak havoc and ultimately destroy a trader.

I tell traders all over the world that trading is 10 percent skill and 90 percent emotion. I am convinced life is 10 percent what happens to me and 90 percent the attitude I maintain to react to the 10 percent that happens to me. However, the 90 percent attitude I choose, good or bad, positive or negative, will have the largest impact and outcome for my life. Your attitude is the control center of your life.

If you don't take charge of your attitude, your life circumstances and events will do it for you, whether they are good or bad. A happy person is not a lucky person who has a certain set of incredible circumstances, but rather a person with a certain set of incredible attitudes. They are not the ones complaining that roses have thorns; they are the ones who are thankful that thorns have roses. I lived in Arizona, and my mom used to say, "Reach for the stars, son, even if you have to stand barefoot on a cactus." Every day when we wake up, we have to make that choice and then begin to address the challenges of the day with that positive or negative attitude. We are the ones in control of our lives, not our circumstances.

The attitude with which we approach life will overall be the same attitude we will approach trading with. If in life you honestly feel that you deserve the best, that you were born to succeed and enjoy the most this life has to offer, that failure is not an option, that success and happiness are the only options for you, then you have placed yourself in a great position to succeed, not only in life but also in trading. The greatest discovery of my trading career is that traders can alter their trading results by altering their attitude.

Traders can alter their trading results by altering their attitude.

Understanding Your Intellect, Talent, and Attitude

Most of us have natural talent in something. Dr. Thomas Armstrong wrote a book, *The 7 Kinds of Smart*, in which he points out that there are seven different types of intellect: word smart, picture smart, music smart, logic smart, people smart, and self-smart. For example, professional singers have an abundance of music intellect, athletes have body smarts, and presidents of companies have an abundance of logic intellect.

What kind of smarts or intellect do you have an abundance of? What are your inherent talents and strengths? It is imperative to think about this because part of our success in life comes from understanding our own intellect and using our smarts by harmonizing them to help us achieve our success.

Most successful traders started off focusing on learning everything they needed to learn to become a successful trader. They then began believing and concentrating on their success, and finally unconsciously or subconsciously developed and merged their logic with their intelligence, like a beautifully harmonized song. However, you cannot sing your way to success as a trader. If you don't know what is driving your performance, how will you know what you need to do differently to improve your potential for success?

There are many people who have not been fortunate enough to have been raised by the most positive caregivers or by people who believed in them. *Children learn what they live from their parents, caregivers, and family.* The fact is that what we have been taught, we do. Sometimes adults have to start all over again, figuring out what they want out of life or what life in general is all about. We have to learn how to give what we never received. Perhaps our caregivers passed on what is called a poison pedagogy; the cruel mindset of "All the incapabilities that I have as a parent, I want to make sure you get them, too."

How sad that many of us come from caregivers who constantly beat us up with a negative reinforcement of a you-can't-do-that attitude, a reinforcement of incapability instead of capability, constant disapproval versus approval, and constant criticism versus constant love. Regardless of our past, if we have not resolved past conflict with someone, there is one factor that can make a difference and change everything: our positive attitude. If we instead fall back into a negative attitude, we will not be trading, or living, to our fullest possible abilities.

Consequences of a Negative Attitude

Let's look at some of the consequences in choosing to live your life with a negative attitude:

- **Your outlook on just about everything is pessimistic.** It really won't matter what your challenges or opportunities are for the day, you will see them as a hovering dark cloud and create all kinds of reasons why they can't be achieved.
- **You close your mind.** You consciously walk around with a chip on your shoulder, and most everything you experience during the day is accompanied by a negative emotion. When you choose to let your negative emotions control your actions, you cut yourself off from the left side of the brain, that is, your knowledge and recall of the benefits of a positive attitude. Your decision-making process then becomes cloudy.
- **Your vision becomes narrow and myopic.** A pessimist sees the difficulty in every opportunity; an optimist sees the opportunity in every difficulty.
- **You emit negative energy.** If you always seem to be downcast, others around you may feel the same way as a result. Negative energy calls forth more negative energy, which creates more negative circumstances and negative events in your life.
- **You are generally unhappy, and most people won't want to be around you.** Everyone has their own struggles in life, and they aren't looking to surround themselves with other miserable people. Rather, they want to be around people who are positive and give them a glimmer of hope.
- **You feel fainthearted, disillusioned, dejected, mad, frustrated, and cheated.** These emotions create a negative attitude, and you feel you have no opportunities. If opportunity were to knock at your door at this point, you probably wouldn't recognize it anyway. You set yourself up for failure.
- **A negative attitude attacks your health.** Doctors and scientists now firmly believe that 75 percent of all sickness and disease start in the mind, resulting from a negative attitude. Researchers have also proven that stress, which starts in the mind, is the number one cause of all fatigue and illness.

Help me understand how any of the preceding points will help you become successful at trading. If any of these consequences sound familiar, then you need to develop a plan to change your attitude, grow a backbone, and fight back against your negative mentality.

You must have a positive attitude to thrive in today's perform-or-perish, results-driven market. It is necessary to learn how to outsmart, outproduce, outperform, and outthink this market every step of the way. A negative attitude will not get you there. It's not that times are changing; it's that the times *have* changed. What worked in the past is not working today, and technology is advancing so rapidly that if we don't have a positive attitude advancing with it, we will be left behind.

> You must have a positive attitude to thrive in today's perform-or-perish, results-driven market.

Problem solving and trading with a negative attitude shut down your left brain. If you shut down your left brain, the challenges and obstacles in life and trading will look bigger. If you maintain a positive attitude and keep your left brain open, however, challenges and obstacles in life and trading will look smaller.

Positive Attitude for Life and Trading

With a negative attitude, you have negative emotions. With a positive attitude, you have positive emotions. To be successful at trading, you need a positive attitude with positive emotions. Combined, they will strongly influence your trading capability and trading results. A healthy, positive attitude is contagious, but don't wait to catch it from others—be the carrier.

All traders have abilities and powers they are not even aware of. We are all born with these abilities and talents, but in most cases, the majority don't know how to go about uncovering, accessing, and mastering them. Instead, we go through life trying different things and hoping to get lucky, but we never really seem able to zero in on any aptitude that can make a dramatic difference in our lives. We don't stick with things long enough to exhaust all possible resources. If something doesn't work within the first few tries, we give up and end up missing out on what could have been our greatest talent and discovery.

One of the reasons I love teaching students from countries outside the United States, especially from third-world countries, is because they take the lessons about trading seriously and learn from them. Some of them do not have the options we do in the United States. If something seems to not work out here in the United States, we conveniently move to another idea or try something new. In third-world countries, if learning to trade does not work out, they usually don't have another option. Therefore, failure is not an option, because it could take years for another opportunity to come along.

Forex might be one of your financial dreams. If so, it requires education, skill, ongoing discipline, and a list of successful habits to reach that dream—not the same old ones you have been subconsciously using and have stood in your way of achieving the financial success you have always dreamed of, but new ones. You must do the following:

- Be committed to living a balanced life.
- Exercise to keep your mind fresh and alert.
- Continue to educate yourself about yourself and your profession.
- Create goals for direction and accomplishment.
- Strive for excellence in everything you do, and especially in your profession.
- Stay focused on the reward of delayed gratification versus your instant gratification.
- Have a personal constitution and be disciplined to your beliefs.
- Always allow yourself the ability to change your negative, destructive thoughts into positive, constructive thoughts.
- Think before you speak, and think before you act.

- Always tell the truth, and more important, be honest with yourself.
- Never give up; rather, persist until you succeed.

There is no greater feeling than knowing you have paid a price for something you accomplished that was worthwhile and will enhance your life forever. In itself, that will participate in creating a daily positive attitude.

How important is a positive attitude to you in your life and your success both in general and in trading? A positive attitude does much more than just turn on the lights in our world; it seems to magically connect us to all sorts of incredible opportunities that are somehow unseen with a negative attitude. Alternatively, if you trade with a negative attitude, you limit your capabilities and set yourself up for failure.

> If you trade with a negative attitude, you limit your
> capabilities and set yourself up for failure.

Researchers have proven that people who have a positive attitude or incorporate positive thinking achieve more and live better, healthier lives. Why? Because the subconscious mind puts to work all the necessary faculties and decision-making processes for a positive outcome.

Unfortunately, most people think all they need to do is set goals, plan ahead, manage their time better, say some daily affirmations, become more disciplined, work with a daily planner, and so on. I wish it were that simple. That mindset is completely wrong and usually causes more grief and frustrations from expectations not being met as you work to achieve your goals. No doubt, the foregoing is part of the formula for financial success, but the bigger part of the formula is the attitude we use to execute our daily tasks and that gets us to our goals.

Think for a moment. What's one big difference between successful people and unsuccessful people? Attitude! Mental attitude is more important than mental capacity. Most successful people are optimistic. It is better to be an optimist who is sometimes wrong than a pessimist who is always right. Optimists move forward knowing they are going to make mistakes, of which they will acquire information that will lead them to success; pessimists move forward in fear of making mistakes. In the end, pessimists will usually create choices from two evils and end up choosing both. To me, optimists really aren't sure whether life is one big tragedy or one big comedy; either way, they really don't care because they are just tickled pink to be in the play. Optimists don't complain about the force of the wind or its direction; they stay focused on adjusting their sails, enabling them to always reach their destination.

> It is better to be an optimist who is sometimes
> wrong than a pessimist who is always right.

Most unsuccessful people never get their mind working for them with a positive attitude. Instead, they get their mind to work against them, creating things they don't want. Your mind and subconscious mind mentally create everything in your life before it is all manifested physically. The attitude used, as you begin to execute it, physically determines the outcome. If the only concept you grasp from this book is that a positive attitude is everything to you and your financial and emotional future, then I have achieved my goal.

Human beings can alter their lives by altering their attitudes. Negative or destructive thoughts are the weeds that choke out the productive seeds in our life that give us definite purpose. Positive thoughts develop positive and dynamic personalities. Negative thoughts develop negative personalities and call forth more negatives in our lives.

Law of Attraction

One concept that changed my life and I believe can change your life is the law of attraction. The law of attraction states: what we think about radiates out of our being and creates circumstances and events that align with what we think about. When we think negative thoughts, we create a negative attitude. That attitude sends out negative vibes to create negative circumstances and events, which ultimately attract negative people who can hurt us. However, when we think positive thoughts, we create a positive attitude. That attitude sends out positive vibes to create positive circumstances and events, which ultimately attract positive people who can help us.

From experience I have discovered that the law of attraction is every bit as consistent as the law of gravity. Wherever you are in the world, if you let go of a glass you are holding in your hand, it will fall to the ground. I have experienced this law of attraction in my life, and I can testify to its consistency. I have been teaching the law of attraction to traders for more than 10 years, and the ones who implement the discipline to take total control of their mind before trading are the ones who walk away with more profits than those who allow their negative emotions to take control of them.

I teach a masters class for advanced Forex traders. My focus is to take experienced traders to the next level. I am there to break their current mindset and free them from their mental incarceration that making 100 pips a week is acceptable. I challenge them with the question, "If the sky is the limit, why then are there footprints on the moon?" I teach them trading methodologies that allow them to make 300-plus pips a day and then walk them through the mental disciplines necessary to accomplish such a task. I not only teach them, but also trade with them live in the market. I teach them a new way of thinking, free them mentally from the bonds of mediocrity, and give them a new standard of trading.

If the sky is the limit, why then are there footprints on the moon?

There are 86,400 seconds in a day. The human mind thinks approximately 70,000 different thoughts a day. That is an average of one thought every 1.2 seconds. When a negative, bad, or destructive thought pops into your mind, implement the discipline to change the thought from negative to positive. You have the power to change negative thoughts to positive thoughts.

As you learn to trade and incur trading scars, don't become bitter, become better. Don't become a victim, become a victor. No successful traders are whiners, they are winners. By constantly being on guard with your thoughts while trading, you can quickly change your negative thoughts to positive ones. With discipline, you will start to improve every facet of your trading existence. It will not make you self-conscious in its negative sense or neurotic; rather, it will lead you to greater awareness, self-control, and freedom from the undesired, random negative thoughts.

In other words, with the right attitude and the right persistence you can consciously and subconsciously do anything or manage anything to success. People love other people with a positive attitude. They will travel to the ends of the earth to find them, and once they find a positive person, they hang onto that person and try hard to be around that person as much as possible. They see positive people as battery rechargers. For some reason, people feel better about themselves when they are around positive people—they see their future as brighter. When they discuss their life surprises and problems with a positive person, they acquire more hope about their own future because positive people live an overall happier life. Negative people do the opposite.

Conclusion

Our challenge begins by practicing awareness of our thoughts during the course of the day. When you watch your thoughts, you'll find many thoughts arising that you don't like or are not constructive. If you want to be successful, you will want to change such thoughts. You can, however, change only those thoughts that you are *aware* of.

To become aware, start thinking about what you are thinking about. That is what successful people do. They get up every morning with a positive attitude and go about their day subconsciously doing what they trained their mind to do. They are performing on automatic, controlling their thoughts and thinking endlessly about their dreams, goals, wants, and desires. They have a positive attitude focused on that distant star, slowly moving toward it until that star's gravity takes over and draws them in with no ability to turn back, forcing them to ultimately experience their desired dream. When we control our mind, we allow our mind to control our actions and thus our actions control our destiny.

CHAPTER 12

LEARNING PATIENCE AND SELF-CONTROL TO AVOID TEMPTATION

Patience is the ability to count down before you blast off. How can traders practice patience in the market when so much of their life speeds along at a mind-blurring pace? As our lives become busier, our commute becomes longer, our schedules become fuller, and our time becomes more valuable. We are catered to by society with more instant, quick, and accommodating services available, promising to bring more pleasure, comfort, entertainment, or efficiency into our lives. Today we have instant mashed potatoes, frozen microwave dinners, fast-food restaurants, drive-through windows, online shopping, drive-through car washes, treadmills, movies on demand, online dating, chairs that recline and massage your whole body, dishwashers, washing machines and dryers, little gizmos that are battery operated and sweep your kitchen floor for you, and cars that self-park. We have instant messaging, cell phones, texting, Bluetooth, AirCards and Wi-Fi, FaceTime, Skype, and Facebook. We have become pretty spoiled. The problem with human beings is they want what they want when they want it.

> Patience is the ability to count down before you blast off.

Patience is the willingness, ability, and capacity to:

- Wait however long it takes to carry out a task, especially one that is boring
- Not easily become frustrated or angry when things you are waiting for don't start to go your way
- Not show anger in situations where the other person is unreasonable
- Be virtuous
- Tap into your experiences and exercise wisdom in decision making
- Endure hardship or inconvenience
- Show self-control and a willingness to tolerate delay

A Study on Patience

Through a study he began in 1960, Stanford University psychologist Michael Mischel demonstrated to the world the importance of patience, the rewards associated with not succumbing to temptations, and even the importance of delayed gratification, which is the ability to wait to obtain something that you want, understanding that the delay will yield an even greater reward.

He took hungry four-year-old children, one at a time, and invited them into a room to talk. Hidden cameras were set up to film the entire event and the children's behavior. He had previously placed a bag of marshmallows on a table with two chairs in the center of the room where he would sit and talk with the child. After chatting for a few minutes the conversation, of course, would gravitate toward asking the child if he or she liked marshmallows. Then upon cue, he would tell the child he had to run an errand that would take about 15 to 20 minutes. He told the child that he or she had a choice of either having one marshmallow right then or waiting for him to return and getting two marshmallows at that time. To a four-year-old who is hungry and has no concept of time, 15 minutes could feel like an eternity.

His study focused on demonstrating a controlled response, or delayed gratification. He tested the children's ability to have patience to wait for the greater reward (delayed gratification) or to indulge right away with a smaller reward. Those who could wait the 15 to 20 minutes would be rewarded with twice as much as those who accepted the reward right away. His study showed that one-third of the children accepted the one marshmallow right away and indulged before he even left the room, one-third broke into the bag and took a marshmallow while he was gone, but one-third patiently waited for him to return so they could receive the two marshmallows.

Part of Michael Mischel's study was to follow those same children for approximately the next 30 years and monitor their activities and achievements as they grew from childhood into adulthood. As he monitored them, he categorized them into two groups called the grabbers and the resisters. The personality, character, and habit differences between the two groups were dramatic: the resisters were more patient, more positive, self-motivating, more persistent in the face of difficulty, able to not succumb to temptation, and able to delay their gratification in pursuit of their goals, while the grabbers were the complete opposite. The resisters over time had acquired disciplined habits of successful people, which resulted in higher incomes, leadership positions, greater career satisfaction, more successful and happier marriages, better health, and more fulfilling lives than the grabbers and even the majority of the population. The grabbers were lower income, indecisive, mistrustful, less self-confident, less satisfied in their jobs, and more troubled and stubborn; they also were challenged in their relationships, which resulted in unsuccessful marriages, poor health, and frustrating lives. Throughout their lives, the grabbers constantly struggled with patience and the ability to acquire the skill of delayed gratification.

What is your personality style, that of a grabber or a resister? The concepts of delayed versus instant gratification are undoubtedly one of the most important choices that separate rich thinking from poor thinking. It certainly is the difference between success and failure at trading.

What is your personality style, that of a grabber or a resister?

Patience and Delayed Gratification in Trading

In my most recent masters class, I was mentoring 12 advanced traders, aiming to help them attain higher levels of achievement. After two days of intense training, discussing new trading methodologies as well as emotional skills and traits, we entered the market live with their real trading accounts. I told everyone where to get in the market, where to reverse our positions if the market did not go our way, and where we would get out for a profit. We would be in these trades for 6 to 10 hours.

Regardless of the trading plan already created, I allowed each trader to do what he or she thought was best for him- or herself. During this time, it was incredibly interesting to observe that all the traders, though taught the same rules, methodologies, and winning habits and concepts they must exercise to achieve their ultimate goal as a master trader, quickly reverted back to their emotional predispositions when it came time to trade, coming up with incredibly different results.

Most traders are already locked into automatic subconscious, destructive, emotional trading habits that stand in the way of their success, and as the market starts to move against them, they begin to jump ship and take losses. Some traders get out with losses, and then when they perceive the market to be turning around, they impatiently jump back in only to take additional losses from chasing it. There are as many different trading actions as there are different traders, of which the majority self-destruct. In talking with the traders who incurred losses, I have discovered that the majority are challenged in truly believing that the original laid-out trading plan will work and they let their impatience get the best of them. That lack of belief coupled with perceived fear of potential loss is what forces them to bail out and lose money.

Inevitably, in every class when we finish our trading day, there will always be just one or two traders who displayed their emotions correctly and acted out the traits of disciplined, emotionally intelligent traders.

Patience and delayed gratification are some of your greatest assets to becoming successful. Impatience means you will need to trade at least twice. The money lost due to the lack of patience forces you to make multiple trades that may or may not work out.

In the end you lose time and money. In any contest between impatience and patience, impatience will win. Regardless of how much patience traders have, they would rather not use it. Impatience at trading is a bad habit that takes money out of your trading account. I have learned it is better to be out of a trade and patiently waiting and wishing to be in, than to be in a trade impatiently waiting and wishing you were out!

Patience in trading is the ability to do the following:

- Sit back and patiently wait for an expected outcome without experiencing anxiety, tension, or frustration.
- Let go of your need for immediate gratification.
- Accept your human imperfections and frailty in the pursuit of your goal or financial success.
- Accept the setbacks that are created from the lack of emotional and technical skills.
- Believe in the concept of never giving up, with an attitude of permanence to your dream.
- Maintain a commitment to learn how to trade with calm, calculated, and considerate actions.
- Find people who can help you, and hang on to those relationships, especially as trouble arises that may take some time to resolve.
- Feel peace, contentment, and satisfaction that you are on the path of financial recovery or increase, and personal growth.

- Curb your enthusiasm, energy, exuberance, and excitement after you have experienced a winning trade. Stay focused on acquiring new information or insight for your next successful trade. Do not become overconfident, for pride comes before a fall.
- Accept that there is no need to rush yourself in this learning curve, that overnight reformations rarely last long, and that gradual change and growth have a greater durability. Remember, this is not a sprinting race, this is a marathon.
- Feel relaxed and calm as you trade on a daily basis, keeping full access to the left side of your brain, which is where your logic and memory reside.
- Buy into the concept that the human life learns line upon line, precept upon precept, and here a little, there a little. Believe that your day-to-day efforts and sacrifices are building a new you, a whole new person with successful skills and traits that create healthy self-esteem.

If you are impatient in trading, you are running the risk of:

- Always being dissatisfied, upset, and angry at the market or yourself for your slow pace of making money or slow growth and change
- Easily losing your emotional control and your temper, and firing off outbursts of anger and blame
- Quickly discarding relationships and becoming a member of the throwaway generation—maybe even throwing away your desire to make it as a trader
- Turning off others in your life who want to support you, but whom you offend by accusing them, when your progress is slow, of "not helping you enough"
- Ignoring all of the positive gains you have made as you learn to trade and only concentrate on what has not yet been accomplished
- Wasting energy fretting and worrying about how slow your progress is going, instead of directing that energy toward the

progress you are making and the productive changes you are making

- Withdrawing prematurely from trying to become a successful trader, because you are not seeing an immediate payoff for your efforts
- Looking for a get-rich-quick scheme that becomes that unsuccessful rainbow chase
- Becoming pessimistic about trading, seeing only the "glass half empty" rather than the "glass half full"
- Losing the ability to reward or reinforce any level of success or attainment, discouraging yourself in the pursuit of your trading dream
- Losing the ability to take your large goal of becoming a great trader and break it down into manageable increments
- Becoming overwhelmed by the large tasks ahead of you, and losing the hope and motivation to keep on trying
- Burning yourself out in the pursuit of instant gratification.

Traders who can develop patience while trading can ultimately achieve what they want. One moment of patience when trading may ward off great disaster or financial loss. One moment of impatience may wipe out your trading account and destroy your attitude, not allowing you to be emotionally prepared for the next trade.

One moment of impatience may wipe out your trading account.

The real secret to being patient as you trade is to find something else to do in the meantime. Human beings love to be productive and busy. We wake up every morning, get dressed, and get ready to tackle the world; however, when it comes to trading, tackling the world can mean patiently waiting for perhaps a few hours for a setup. The problem lies in the fact that human beings don't want to wait, don't like to wait, hate being patient, and want to get going.

With trading, patience is a form of action and needs to be put into perspective. Patience is not passive; on the contrary, it is very active because it consists of concentrated strength. Patience is the companion to wisdom. You must work on it, as it is not acquired overnight. It is like building a muscle; every day you have to take the time to exercise it and work on it. To have a lot of patience, you have to practice. Patience with delayed gratification is worth more than cleverness.

Most traders fail to realize that patiently waiting is part of a trader's job. Our patience as traders will achieve more than our impatience, as impatience forces a bad trade. Most traders think waiting creates fatigue, fatigue creates impatience, and impatience forces a trade. To a trader, a forced trade creates frustration, and frustration gets you to do things you normally would not do if you did not have to wait so long. In the end, impatient traders ultimately take a loss in their trades, and a series of financial losses will destroy any trader's dream.

Learning and Listening to the Language

When it comes time to trading, patience allows you to listen to the market properly. In my book *The 10 Essentials to Forex Trading*, I focus on the secret language of the marketplace and the importance of learning the language of Japanese candlesticks. The markets speak a secret language. It is one of the most amazing skills you will learn, enabling you to financially take advantage of the Forex market. As you learn this skill, it is like learning sign language that enables you to communicate with a person who is deaf. The reality is that the market is deaf; however, it is not mute. It communicates and will communicate what it is going to do via Japanese candlestick sign language; you just need to be patient to see what it has to say.

As you learn the skill of reading Japanese candlesticks, you need to envision yourself as having a conversation with the market. You will be asking the market a question, "Is it time for me to get in?" When it responds with no candlestick formation, that is your answer to stay out. If it responds with a candlestick formation, that is your answer to get in. The big question is, are you a patient, good listener or an impatient, bad listener? A bad listener controls and forces a conversation. Bad listeners who takes their bad listening habits to the trading table and try to control the conversation with the market will be humiliated, shamed, and beat up by the market in the end. Good listeners who take their good listening habits to the trading table will have the knowledge and patience to ask the right question and patiently wait for the answer. This allows them to enter into a productive, healthy, and wonderful conservation with the market and to profit in the end. Good conversationalists have mastered the art of patiently waiting until everything is said before they respond.

Say it is time to trade and you ask the question, "Is it time for me to get in?" If the answer is yes, it is because you have educated yourself about how the market works and you will start to see a series of things that say it is time to get in. For example, the market will be bouncing at a trend line, breaking a counter trend line, bouncing at a Fibonacci retracement number, bouncing at past resistance, becoming future support, and finally forming a bullish candlestick formation. When the market responds with those answers and you know what you are doing, you have a high percentage chance at being successful in your trade.

Learning this new language can give you a different perspective and vision on trading. It can place you at a huge advantage. Learning this language and developing the patience for the right answers can allow you to develop a new financial career. Trading is not complex; we as human beings are complex. We make trading difficult. Trading is relatively simple and believe it or not, it is the clear and simple trading technique that is the right thing to do.

Temptation in Trading

There is a Mexican saying that goes, "Step by step we end up walking a long way." Too many people don't understand the importance of delayed gratification. They demand instant gratification. That mindset creates a big problem for traders. Why? Because the overwhelming majority need to get it now, to achieve it now, and to become rich now is a negative mindset that places the trader in a position to become impatient and succumb to the feelings of temptation while trading.

The definition of *temptation* is "something that seduces or has the quality to seduce; the desire to have or do something that you know you should avoid." For example, "He felt the temptation to get in the market. He was being enticed by the movement of the market when the entry was totally against his rules or disciplines. His enticements were shameless. His willpower weakened." Temptation is the act of influencing by exciting hope or desire.

Temptation is an appealing desire to go against your constitution. For a trader, it is a state of mental conflict between what we believe to be right and what we believe to be wrong. If seduced and succumbed to, the temptation turns into a shameless act and is considered a trader's sin. As such, temptation tends to lead a trader to regret such actions due to the feeling of guilt. Guilt usually comes in later to kick us when we are down and already suffering from the painful consequence. Guilt is the "I told you so!" when we are already painfully aware of the mistake we made. However, it seems that without pain, guilt, and sorrow, there is no lesson to be learned.

What happens to most new traders as they are learning to trade is they see the market moving in all kinds of directions. They say to themselves, "Boy, if I would have gotten in there, look at all the money I could have made." True, if they had entered in there, they would have made all that money, but the reality is, they wouldn't have entered in there, because they hadn't been taught yet how to get in there.

Learning to successfully trade is a process, not a onetime event. As traders are learning to trade, they are slowly creating their trader's value system or trader's constitution. The process they go through is no different than the process we all go through growing up. Imagine going through life with no one teaching you anything. You can't talk to anyone; you can only feel your way around through trial and error. I would say there would be a high probability you wouldn't make it past five years old, if that. Imagine working your way through the market with no help from anyone. How well would you do? How long would you last?

Good habits are formed from resisting temptation. They are there to keep you safe. Every trader who is taught how to trade and then disobeys the rules has succumbed to some form of temptation. That desire to break tried-and-true trading rules is called temptation. All productive trading rules need to be written on your tablet of stone labeled "Trading Rules and Disciplines." They are there to keep you safe.

Good habits are formed from resisting temptation.
They are there to keep you safe.

There is nothing wrong with being creative and experimenting with something new. That in itself is another process. If you do that, do it on a demo account. Make sure it has a history of success, and whatever you do, attach a set of rules you are willing to obey for your newfound methodology.

When you succumb to the temptation of getting in the market due to a hunch or a feeling, or just because (and you ignore your trading methodology), and it rewards you with 100, 200, 300, maybe even 500 pips in that trade, the toughest discipline you have to overcome when you get that feeling or hunch again is to not concede to temptation again and repeat that action. Even though it paid you, successful trading is about learning trading methodologies or market setups that have a high percentage of payout, perhaps a setup that has an 80 percent track record of success versus a setup that has only a 20 percent track record of success. Even a setup that has a 20 percent chance of success still has a chance of success; however, it also has an 80 percent chance of failure, and those are not the trades you want to be taking, because they lose more than they ever win.

Over time, you will learn that feelings and hunches will disappoint you and financially hurt you much more than they will help you. You need to correct your thought processes about your hunch-driven actions and purge those feelings out of the deep and locked chambers of your subconscious mind, heart, and memory bank.

When you are tempted to break rules in your life that you know you should not be breaking and the event turns out to be a wonderful experience, you will fight for the rest of your life to not want to do that again. If the experience turns out to be disastrous or you get busted, not only will you regret that the rest of your life, but you will have to work the rest of your life changing and rebuilding your reputation. You can be tempted to do something in an instant that will give you heartache for years to come, something stupid or greedy that will wipe out your entire trading account in hours.

Thousands of traders crash and burn each day in the valleys of temptation, incurring irreparable damage because they allowed themselves to get caught up in their fantasies of how the market would turn their financial world around. They strayed off course because of their unwillingness to create a solid trading foundation, that is, a sound trading strategy accompanied with a plan of action that they would be willing to obey.

The biggest temptation most traders fight is the temptation to settle for too little. Some traders succumb to the temptation of settling for too little. They are content with 10 pips a day when the market is willing to give them substantially more. Perhaps if traders walk away with 10 pips a day consistently, they could consider themselves somewhat successful. Every trader must find a balance between settling for too little and wanting too much. The bigger temptation of the two is the temptation of greediness, where you are always wanting more and your modest yield for the day is simply not enough. Most of us pretty much know what we want to do, what we want to be, and what we want to get out of trading. Yet, we have a hard time getting there because we too often or occasionally succumb to temptation.

The biggest temptation most traders fight with
is the temptation to settle for too little.

Overcoming temptation then must become a learned and skilled habit, one of programmed default. When we make and enforce a good habit, we are liberating ourselves from enslavement to negative behavior. No time is wasted on sorrow, guilt, or pain. Your focus is placed on obedience and reaping the benefits of that obedience. Your view of the market starts to open up, and things begin to become clearer. You see that little-by-little you are becoming free and can now start to see the light at the end of the tunnel.

Here are 10 steps to help you overcome your temptation in trading:

1. Immediately walk through the worst thing that can happen to you if you succumb to the temptation. Address the downside should things not work out. What will you ultimately lose financially? Ask yourself if it will be worth the loss.
2. Challenge your thoughts, and ask the question, "What's in it for me?" By questioning the temptation, you will have the opportunity to correct the errors in your thinking and make changes. In addition, it will keep you from acting impulsively.
3. Remove the exciting symbolic hook of making a lot of money on this trade from your brain. Temptation gains power and momentum by attaching itself to an emotion. Instead of thinking about all that money you are going to make if this trade pays off, think of the pain you will feel if it doesn't.
4. Don't buy into the trap of promising yourself you will do what is right next time. When you disregard the alert you have been given, you dull your conscience. The alarm becomes quieter with time, and you will repeat the offense. Soon it may be so quiet that you will neglect to hear it at all.
5. Replace your thoughts of the instant gratification that create the temptation with more logical thoughts of delayed gratification or the big picture. Become bulletproof.

6. Step back and think before you act. Don't let your emotions control your actions. You know the right thing to do: control your emotions. You know that when you prefer acting on your emotions rather than your value system, you will lose more than you will ever gain.

7. Apply your common sense to the situation before you act. If you don't see a setup, your common sense should say, "You are involved with a low percentage trade, so pass on the trade and wait until a high percentage trade sets up."

8. If you cannot find your setup in the time frame or currency you need, look for a setup in another currency and another time frame that meets the criteria of your trading rules. Don't just stare at one currency. Staring at just one currency will create boredom, and boredom opens the door to temptation.

9. When there is not a setup, do not force one; stay busy doing something else like reading and continuing to educate yourself about the market.

10. Last, be very clear on the differences between instant gratification and delayed gratification as well as on where you stand with the two of them.

In your life, how many times did you have to do something twice because you did not have the patience to wait and you succumbed to the temptation to just do it? You were in such a hurry, you did a sloppy job at it and now guess what? You get to do it over again. Impatience becomes a destructive trading habit.

Conclusion

A handful of patience is far more valuable than a barrel of brains. Consider the hourglass; you cannot speed up its process and nothing can be accomplished by shaking or rattling it. You must patiently wait until each grain of sand passes through the funnel from one chamber to the next. Patience can't be acquired overnight. It is just like building up a muscle. You need to work on it every day.

One key to trading is having the patience to wait for the setup. Patience is power, and our patience will achieve more than force: you get the chicken by hatching the egg, not by smashing it. As they say in Turkey, "Patience is the key to paradise." Financial gain along with wisdom are the rewards you get for properly listening to the market and patiently waiting for the right setup, instead of telling the market what it should do for you. Never forget the golden rule in trading: Think before you act! Ask first, listen second, execute with confidence. Ready, aim, fire!

CHAPTER 13

LISTENING WITH HUMILITY

Listening with humility is the crown of the noble. There is an Argentine proverb that says, "He who speaks, sows; he who listens, reaps." Listening is everything in trading. If you can't listen to people in life, how do you expect to pick up the skill of listening to the charts? *Listening* means possessing an awareness and openness in learning something new.

To listen fully means to pay close attention to what is being said behind the words or even the charts. In trading, you listen not only to the charts but also to the essence of what they are saying—it is the art of developing deeper silences in yourself so you can slow your mind's hearing to your ears' natural speed and hear what is being said behind the charts.

> Listen not only to the charts but also to the
> essence of what they are saying.

The charts talk, and in most cases we refuse to listen to what they are saying and we do what we want regardless of what they are saying. We get in when they are screaming stay out; we stay out when they are screaming get in. We respond that way because we don't listen to truly understand or to truly learn. The majority of the world is busy talking with no one listening, and they take that habit to the trading table. When you become so busy trying to tell the charts what they are going to do rather than listening to what the charts are telling you they will do, you will lose. When you've learned the art of listening you've learned just about everything you need to know in your life and in your trading career to start to turn things around.

If in all our practices of life we could learn to listen, if we could just grasp and acquire the habit of listening to what other people are saying as they themselves understand what they are saying, and if we could bring that trait, skill, or habit to the trading table, we would succeed.

Listening Versus Hearing

There is a big difference between listening and hearing. Hearing is acknowledging that someone else is talking, and this usually implies you are waiting for the instant he or she pauses to take a breath so you can jump in and take over the conversation. Listening, however, is understanding and comprehending what someone else is saying. It is more than just hearing the words and facts a person is saying; it is catching the essence and heart of what was said. It is grasping the insight behind the words spoken. If you are really listening, then you ought to be able to repeat back to the person the content of what was just said with factual accuracy, relaying the emphasis and passion with exactness and precision. This task is difficult and means you really need to be focusing hard. But this is what true listening resembles. Effective listeners remember that words have no meaning; people have meaning.

Stop Talking and Start Listening

When you talk less, you automatically learn more—you hear more, see more—and make fewer costly mistakes. When you stop listening, you stop learning. You stop looking for things to understand, and you stop asking questions.

FILTERING AGENTS

Among the most influential operating factors during the process of listening and communicating are the filtering agents of senders and receivers. Similar to filters used with a camera lens, filtering agents allow the passage or blockage of coloring elements to the film. Consider how professional photographers use filters designed to let in some rays of light while screening out other rays that may ruin or distort a picture. While a filter is in use, it becomes a part of the camera and affects the final outcome of the picture.

Camera filters are changed to get desired results. Similar to a camera lens, filter agents are used in communicating not only with others but also with trading charts. Filtering agents such as past work experiences, educational training, opinions, emotions, attitudes, and feelings influence how you communicate. Understanding your personal filtering agents puts you in a position to maximize your communication and listening success.

When being taught a new concept, new skill, or any type of information in a class or other learning environment, the human mind wanders 5.4 times every 45 minutes.[1] It is not quantified for how long the minds of people wander, but it is likely that their minds are off worrying about problems they are currently facing, thinking about things they need to get done, or daydreaming about something else. With people having wandering minds, you would think they would need to listen to what they are being taught a minimum of four times to start to fully understand the concepts or information. Even then they might not fully under-

---

1. Carl Zimmer, "Stop Paying Attention: Zoning Out Is a Crucial Mental State," *Discover Magazine*, http://discovermagazine.com/2009/jul-aug/15-brain-stop-paying-attention-zoning-out-crucial-mental-state. June 15, 2009.

stand everything they are being taught, because they are not fully listening.

Most people need a definite purpose, a specific reason for listening, otherwise they don't pay attention and don't really hear or comprehend what someone is telling them. Of course, you listen to learn and retain information. The first step to effective hearing and comprehending is to stop talking and start listening.

The first step to effective hearing and comprehending
is to stop talking and start listening.

If we could just learn the consistent habit of talking less and listening more while trading we might become more successful. We can't learn anything when we're talking.

Bracketing

An essential part of true listening is learning the discipline called *bracketing*: the temporary giving up or setting aside of one's own prejudices, frames of reference, and personal desires so as to experience as much as possible the speaker's world from the inside out. The most basic of all human needs is the need to understand and be understood. To be listened to is, generally speaking, a nearly unique experience for most people. It is enormously stimulating. It is a small wonder that people who have been demanding all their lives to be heard so often fall speechless when confronted with someone who solemnly and seriously agrees to lend an ear.

Humility in Listening and Learning

We should never pretend to know what we don't know; we should not feel ashamed to ask and learn from people whom we think are below or above us. We should learn to listen carefully to the opinions and views of those in life whom we feel are not only at the highest levels, but even those at the lowest levels. We can learn something from everybody. Be a pupil before you become a teacher; and learn from every walk of life.

In all aspects of life, humility leads to strength. Humility is like a mature tree, whose roots are deep in the earth, enabling it to rise higher, stand firmer, spread its branches farther, and last longer. It is the highest form of self-respect and the only true way for people to look into themselves. Without taking the time to introspect, you won't take the time to figure out the steps necessary to success. Humility helps you admit mistakes and provides courage to amend them, leading to self-improvement. Just as in all other things in your life, when listening to others, do so with humility and you will learn more.

Destructive Versus Constructive Ego

The majority of the world is confused about the definition of an ego. When they hear the term *ego* they think in terms of destructive and negative, when in fact there are two types of egos, a constructive ego and a destructive ego: the destructive ego is harmful and the constructive ego is productive. A destructive ego is considered the anesthetic that dulls the pain of stupidity. Destructive egos think they were born on third base yet go around telling everyone they just hit a triple. Destructive egos believe this is their world and the rest of us just live in it. They are so caught up in themselves that when they heard that science discovered the center of the universe, they were heartbroken to find out they were not it. They are so naive that they are like the delusional rooster that thinks the sun rises to hear it crow. None are so empty as those who are so full of themselves. They may hear others, but they refuse to listen, because they believe they know all there is to know.

I think it is important to swallow your pride (after all, it is nonfattening). When people consider themselves better than the rest, that is usually the beginning of the end for them. People who believe they can live without others are mistaken. People who think others can't live without them are even more delusional. It is humility that gives a person freedom from a destructive ego and breaks the chains of mediocrity. Humility is the avenue we must take to prepare our minds for all the changes we need to make to reach our highest potential. Humility is nothing but truth and is the only way we will ever get a right judgment or assessment of ourselves. Pride is nothing more than a false assessment of ourselves, filled with lies. Humility is thinking less of yourself rather than thinking of yourself less. It is opening your mind and offering no resistance to change, enabling you to listen and learn what you need to improve your life.

It is humility that gives a person freedom from a destructive ego and breaks the chains of mediocrity.

Without humility we have no humanity. Greatness does not lie in looking down on someone; it lies in only looking down to help a person up. We are highest when we stoop to help. Too many people walk around thinking they are something they are not and overvalue what they think they are. We will all act out what we believe ourselves to be regardless of what we truly are.

Since people act out what they believe themselves to be, regardless of the truth, you must be extremely careful with your self-perception. You must ask, "Is it really a constructive ego I have or destructive ego?" In many cases, that difference becomes the make-you-or-break-you turning point.

Some people are always ready to attack and level those above them and bring them down to themselves. I see it every day. As I give presentations around the world on trading, I never cease to be amazed at how some people were so beat up from childhood about their inabilities and capabilities that they need to take it out on me and try to bring me down to their level. I find it interesting that these types of people are never willing to bring the people below them up to their own level. They constantly walk around blinded by their own assumed greatness and never achieve anything great; they never listen to others or learn. Everyone must realize that life is a long lesson in humility.

Many people believe that humility is the opposite of pride, when in fact, it is a point of equilibrium. The opposite of pride is actually the lack of self-esteem. A person who walks around with humility is a totally different person from the person who cannot recognize who he or she truly is or appreciate him- or herself as one of God's masterpieces. Be not mistaken: humility does not mean weakness. It is positioning yourself to become more aware of realities and potential problems or challenges that can be turned into opportunities in your life. Humility is power.

Great Listeners Make Great Traders

Great traders are great listeners. Whether listening is natural for them or has become a learned skill that turned into a good habit, they know how to listen. As a trader, you must be able to clearly listen to four things:

- **The charts.** They will tell you when it is time to get in and time to get out. You must trade by the charts and not by your heart.
- **Your education.** This includes the logical thoughts from what you have been taught, which are racing through your head as you are watching the charts move in all kinds of directions.
- **Your patience.** It is important to learn to listen to your patience and endure the downtime when a trade is setting up. It is being able to *not* grab the one marshmallow and having the patience to wait for the bag later. Do not forget the importance and benefits of delayed gratification.
- **Your equity management.** Never let your greed exceed your need; otherwise, you will overtrade your account and end your trading dream.

Then there are four things that you should never listen to as a trader:

- **Your impatience.** Most Forex traders want to find a trade and make money in two to four hours, scalping the market. When traders sit down to trade and listen to their impatience, they will force a trade. A forced trade is a losing trade.
- **Your greed.** When traders listens to their greed, they will self-destruct. For when greed exceeds their need, it will take them down a path of self-destruction. It is what I call the traders' "I need it now" disease—there is value in learning to wait for a trade.
- **Your destructive ego.** All great traders must park their destructive ego outside the door of their trading room. They must trade with only the utmost respect of the market. Your pride and arrogance will be your trading downfall.
- **Your heart.** You cannot afford to listen to your emotions as you trade. Trading is not about dealing with your feelings; it is about making a trading plan in a state of logic and unemotionally following that plan.

All great traders must park their destructive ego
outside the door of their trading room.

How many trades have you entered that you wish you had stayed out of, and then after you lost money, you went back only to find out you were not properly listening to the charts? You could have saved a lot of money from listening to the following:

- The trend line
- The candlestick formations
- The harmonic vibrations
- The Fibonacci retracements or extensions
- Your disciplines and rules

You cannot listen to the charts when they are speaking if you are preoccupied with your emotions and feelings or with impressing other people who are anxiously waiting to see your results. You cannot listen to the charts if you are trying to force a trade because of the limited time you have or are debating about whether what you have been taught is really true, relevant, or agreeable. Effective listeners at trading learn that their emotions have no meaning—candlestick formations, trend lines, and the charts do.

> Emotions have no meaning—candlestick
> formations, trend lines, and the charts do.

Listening to Set Up the Trade

The best way to understand people is to listen to them. The best way to understand the market is to learn to listen to it. The opposite of talking is not listening. The opposite of talking is pausing or waiting. And we need to learn how to wait for the setup at trading. Having the patience to listen to the charts, waiting for the market to give the OK to get in or get out becomes one of a trader's greatest challenges.

Adult listening behaviors become habitual. Our listening behaviors have been acquired and reinforced over a long period of time. As adults we rarely think about how we listen or consider that it takes time to change old habits. We listen the way we do because we have learned to listen that way.

Our bad listening habits many times don't allow us to properly communicate, and we take that bad habit to the trading table. Our relationship with the charts is just that—a working relationship of proper communication. The better we listen, the more money we make. The worse we listen, the less money we make. Should you choose to not listen to the charts and to begin to do what you want, enter when you want, and chase the market like you want, then you need to be prepared to get beat up. To communicate with the charts is risky; to not communicate with the charts is riskier. The greatest problem in chart communication is the illusion that you are a great listener when in the end you haven't listened effectively.

Many attempts to communicate in life and with other people are nullified by talking too much and hearing too little. Many attempts to communicate with the charts are nullified by not taking the time to learn the proper sign language of the charts. Learn your trends. Learn your candlestick formations and trend direction from the different time frames. Try to listen carefully to the charts so you do not have to take a financial loss.

Conclusion

Carl Rogers, an influential American psychologist and among the founders of the humanistic approach to psychology, said, "Man's inability to communicate is a result of his failure to listen effectively, skillfully, and with understanding to another person." With that bad habit in your life, you will take that inability to properly listen with you to the charts. You will fail to listen to the charts effectively, skillfully, and with understanding. I have yet to come across a person who listened him- or herself out of a job. And I have yet to come across a trader who went broke from becoming an excellent listener to the charts.

It is a rare person who wants to hear bad news or the opposite of what he or she had hoped for. Think about it. You are patiently waiting for a trade, trying to listen to the charts. You only have four hours to trade, and you really want to make a trade. After all, in your mind, being in the market is the only way to make some money. Remember, it is better to be out of a trade wishing you were in than it is to be in a trade wishing you were out.

You start to get impatient, but the charts say stay out. But that is not what you want to hear. When it says stay out—then stay out, even if that is not what you want to hear. You might save yourself some money, and saving money not trading sometimes becomes the best winning trade you ever execute. It takes more courage to stay out of the market than it does to get into the market at a place you have no business entering.

If you can't humble yourself and listen to what you need to learn about trading, you won't make it. When we stop listening, we stop learning, and when we stop learning we stop progressing!

CHAPTER 14

LEARN TO TRADE
WITH CONFIDENCE

Have you ever felt so confident that it did not matter what you said but you knew that people liked you, they were interested in what you had to say, and you were allowed to be 100 percent yourself? For most people the answer is seldom or *never.* How good would it feel if you were allowed to be your true self, confident about your thoughts and ideas, and you knew you were loved and accepted by others? How good it would feel if you took large profits, winning trades 70 percent of the time and losing only 30 percent of the time, with small losses! Wouldn't that do something for your self-esteem, self-worth, and self-confidence?

The best way to develop self-confidence is to build the courage to address the things you fear most in life. The definition of *courage* is a quality of spirit that enables you to face danger or pain without showing fear; bravery, fortitude, will, and intrepidity; or the ability to confront fear, pain, risk and danger, uncertainty, or intimidation. To be courageous is to do the right thing regardless of its cost; it is a condition of a strong soul rather than of a strong body.

You gain strength, courage, and confidence by every experience in which you really stop to look fear in the face. As a trader, after getting whacked a few times, you must confront your fears and do the thing that you think you cannot: get right back in there and trade. What could be more mortifying than feeling you have missed a good trade because you did not have the courage and the confidence to get in? Courage, after all, isn't the absence of fear; it's the mastery of it.

Confronting Trading Fears with Confidence

Whether a novice or a seasoned trader, everyone feels a level of fear as they trade. What helps take that feeling of fear away is education about the unknown and in the case of the trader, about how the market works. Think back to when you were a little kid and feared the dark. Your rampant imagination told you the bogey monster hid in all dark places, especially your closet. Remember how real the fear felt to you when you were young? Remember how certain you were that the monster existed and that a horrible fate of some sort awaited you if you were left alone in the darkness?

Now take that concept and apply it to fears you have today in your life. For example, you fear losing money in the market. Let's break that down:

- What do you fear about losing money?
- What does that mean to you?
- How does that make you feel?
- What implications will that bring?
- What is the worst-case scenario?
- What is the most-probable-case scenario?

After asking yourself to mentally walk through all the possible options and scenarios, dissect your emotions thoroughly, and completely exhaust all avenues of that one fear, is it really so bad? Would it be so horrible if it actually happened, if you lost money? Do you think all those things *will* really happen if you lose money at trading? If you are a logical person, I'm sure you would answer no to that question.

Would it be so horrible if it actually happened, if you lost money?

Consider other common fears of traders:

- Losing the respect of loved ones, friends, and associates whom they have told that they are trading
- Having their ego attacked by making wrong trading decisions
- Running out of money and entering into a state of desperation
- Flat-out failing at trading and then feeling embarrassed among family and friends

Will life go on if you are forced to deal with the preceding issues?

Whether in our personal life or trading life, we have to look at the things we fear the most; address them, regardless of how scary or painful they may be; and confront them head-on with the attitude that nothing is impossible and everything is solvable. When truth and logic shine light into the dark corners of our mind, they expose fear for what it really is—a toothless monster that can't do anything but stand there and look scary. But until we choose to walk over to it, take out our flashlight, and point the light directly at it, we don't get an accurate picture. Are you going to be the kid who stays in bed, paralyzed with fear, clutching your covers up around your neck, or are you going to start climbing out of bed armed with your flashlight of truth?

What helps take that fear away and build your confidence is education or knowledge about the unknown. As an adult, when fear enters your being, it is usually caused by a potential problem that confronts you, where you have no answer or resolution. When you step back, dissect the problem, and carefully find a resolution, your fear goes away. Since fear can be caused by internal and external sources, courage cannot be measured by an external situation alone. A person's apparent courage may vary greatly from situation to situation. Even the bravest of people have limited endurance under prolonged exposure to fear and pain.

To be successful at trading, you need to address your fear so that whenever you experience what you think is the worst thing that could ever happen, you can look into the mirror and say to yourself, "I lived through that horrible tragedy, and I am still alive.

I didn't lose my life, my family, my house, or my car (and that is what equity management does for you). I am now ready to take the next step." When you say it, you will also need to believe it.

MARKET TRADERS INSTITUTE (MTI) CONTEST

We had a contest at MTI to see who could make the most pips in a given month, trading one lot at a time. The winner made 431 pips; he executed 120 trades for the month. He was wrong 52 percent of the time, yet he walked away making $4,310 at $10 per pip. (Had he traded 10 lots at a time, he would have made $43,100 for the month.) He didn't fear his losses or take them personally. He didn't throw pity parties after each trade he lost. Rather, because of his education on how the market works, he had the courage to get right back up and continue to trade. When giving him his award, I told everyone, "If he can do it, you can do it!"

Experience creates wisdom. Experience is what we gain when we don't get what we want. The grief of failure or the joy of success associated with your trading will create a discipline, a new action that will benefit you. It will either place you in a position of humility where you can better learn from your mistake or error, or bring you a feeling of triumph.

Experience is what we gain when we don't get what we want.

As you embark on your journey as a trader, you will from time to time enter into a fearful environment. It is precisely at that time that you need to step back and go over everything you have learned and return to the basics: assure yourself that you know what you're doing, that you have the training, knowledge, attitude, and ability to succeed.

Rewards of Trading Confidently

Trading is not about having an undefeated trading season. Nor is it about being right 100 percent of the time. It is a game of high percentages going to work against low percentages. You can be wrong 70 percent of the time at trading and still deposit a lot of money in the bank if you understand equity management. For example, if you executed three trades that were right and made $2,000 per trade, the total amount of earned income is $6,000. Now execute seven trades that were wrong and you lost $400 per trade. That adds up to $2,800. Subtract $2,800 from $6,000, and the balance you get to deposit in the bank is $3,200.

It takes courage to become a successful trader, and I strongly commend every trader who tackles the market. If you can make an average of 200 pips per month without stress or fear, you can create a $20,000, $40,000, or $60,000 income per month. The choice is yours based on the amount of lots you trade.

Whatever course you think you need to take to make those 200 to 400 pips a month, you need to make a decision. You need to map out a course of action and follow it to an end. That requires you to have courage. Pulling the trigger 120 times and losing 52 percent of the time to capture 431 pips in a month takes courage.

There is always someone willing to tell you that you are wrong. There are always situations, difficulties, and even financial losses that arise and tempt you to believe your critics are right. However, 431 pips for the month means financial freedom.

Don't try to outguess this market. Don't try to outguess the strength of a trend or your indicators. Create a system or methodology you buy into, and have the courage to follow it. I promise you, you will lose as you trade, and I promise you, you will win as you trade. What you must do is not fear your losses, rather put your losses into perspective.

The greatest test of courage is to incur defeat without losing heart.

What helped me put my trading losses into proper perspective was I started to look at trading as running a business. In running any business, large or small, you will have overhead, paying rent, paying employees, paying the light bill, making lease payments for cars and equipment, paying taxes, and so on. When I started to look at my trading losses as overhead to running a business, I was able to stay more focused on my gains and not complain or worry about my losses. Look at how business owners take pride in paying certain overheads, like their employees' wages. Remember that with every loss that goes by, you are getting that much closer to success. The greatest test of courage is to incur defeat without losing heart.

So you must move forward without giving into that little voice inside you that says, "This isn't for you," "It's too hard," or "You're not a winner, you are a loser. Making $20,000, $40,000, or $60,000 a month is not for you, it is for someone else."

If you don't believe it can happen . . . then your courage is dead. Courage is the capacity to confront what can be imagined. The scars you acquire by exercising courage will never make you feel inferior. They build self-esteem and self-worth. They will make you a stronger, wiser, and better trader.

A Higher Type of Courage

Courage takes on many forms. There is physical courage, moral courage, and emotional courage, but when it comes to trading, there is still a higher type of courage:

- The courage to perform in a state of pain
- The courage to live with that pain as you try to figure out a trading system that works for you
- The courage to keep pressing on as you deal with the pain of financial losses while you confront fear and figure out your system
- The courage to live with it day in and day out with a smile on your face as you never let anyone else know of it or about what you are truly going through

- The courage to not throw a pity party, but still find joy in your day-to-day life after you trade and take a financial hit
- More important, the courage to get up in the morning with the attitude that today you will prevail in your trading after three days of losses

Courage is very important. Like a muscle, it is only strengthened by use.

As you face your fears in trading, you acquire strength, courage, and confidence from every experience that did not go your way. To have courage as part of your trading armor is like acquiring a special kind of inside information that allows you to perform with confidence. Some fear is healthy: by acquiring wisdom, you begin to know the difference between healthy and unhealthy fear. Knowledge of how to fear what ought to be feared (you must fear big losses) and how not to fear what you ought not to fear will set you free.

Simplicity, Confidence, and Courage

To simplify means to have the courage and ability to eliminate the unnecessary so that the necessary may speak.

I have been invited all over the world to work with and mentor traders. I never cease to be amazed when I walk into their offices and see their workspace cluttered with papers in no apparent order, stacked up 6 inches high, with stuff scattered all over their offices to the point you can barely see their computers. It has always been my motto, "A messy desk, a messy mind; a tidy desk, a tidy mind." Simplifying the complications in your life is a leap to success. And what better way to start than with the easiest, most basic things . . . like your office?

It takes courage to get rid of clutter. For some reason we buy things that start out in our house and make their way to the garage, but never make their way to the Salvation Army or the garbage can; they just stay there in our lives gently asking, "What about me, what are you going to do about me? Please pay attention to me. Please deal with me." They become a daily burden.

If you want to trade with a clear head, have nothing in your office or your home that is not useful to you or beautiful and calming to look at. Your workspace should appear serene. Get rid of the rest. You should only have things in your home or office that serve a positive purpose, are useful, and make you feel happy to look at.

Simplicity is making life's journey with as little emotional and physical baggage as possible. We don't need to increase our earthly possessions nearly as much as we need to scale down our wants. Having the desire of not wanting something is far better than possessing it. To be rich may mean having a lot of things, but to be wealthy is to be content with small means, stylishness, and grace rather than extravagance and lavishness, refinement rather than fashion, and worthiness instead of propriety and useless decorum. As Leonardo DaVinci said, "Simplicity is the ultimate sophistication."

If you are presently trading or trying to achieve anything in life and struggling, perhaps your life is much too complicated and needs to be reexamined and reorganized. Free yourself from clutter, and enable your mind to stay focused only on the things that are productive. Simplicity is a learned skill.

Believe it or not, when it comes time to trading, everything is simpler than we can imagine. At the same time, due to our inner desire to make things complicated, everything is more complicated than we can conceive. Very frequently when I teach people the *simple* way of trading, they say, "It can't be that simple." I emphatically tell them, "But it is."

If you had been taught by me to trade 15 years ago, you would have said forget it. I had written 16 books that you had to study and understand before you could trade. Once I started to see that the complexity was hindering the ability to successfully trade, I started dedicating my life to making it simple. Today, 16 books and manuals have been condensed to a couple of pages: a simple map that shows a trader where the gold is. Making the simple complicated is commonplace; everyone does it. The reason we make simple thinking complicated is because it makes us feel important and intelligent. Besides, human beings are always thinking of the what-ifs and asking, "What about this?" The reality is that making the complicated simple, awesomely simple, is not only creativity, it's intelligence. Look at what Bill Gates did. By creating the simple-to-use, easy-to-learn, and easy-to-understand Windows software, he and many others became billionaires.

When you have the courage to start to simplify your life, enabling yourself to focus on the things in your life that matter, that start to serve you well, and that even make you money, your confidence is born. When we start to achieve productive things, we start to feel confident in those things. When we learn to master minor things in our life, we gain confidence to try to master things of greater significance. Start with the small, fundamental things, and watch your confidence and skill grow as you begin to master larger and more significant areas of your life, working your way up to the more challenging and essential things. As the Bible says, "He who is faithful with little will be faithful also with much."

> When you have the courage to start to simplify
> your life, your confidence is born.

Imagine how good it would feel to sit in front of your computer with a sense of confidence in your own trading abilities, being able to be true to yourself and confident about your thoughts and ideas.

Low Self-Esteem

Confidence is self-discipline and self-knowledge. Confidence never comes from having all the answers; it comes from being open to all the questions. Confidence thrives on honesty, honor, the sacredness of obligations, faithful protection, and unselfish performance. Self-confidence is the first prerequisite to great undertakings and personal accomplishments. Confidence is an aura of being sure without being cocky. Confidence has nothing to do with money. Confidence never runs scared.

A *true*, inner self-confidence that stays with you even in stressful situations like trading can only come from changing the way you really think about yourself subconsciously. True self-confidence that stays with you is not only a decision, but the result of how you feel about yourself.

If perhaps you have insecurities or low self-esteem, your self-confidence will easily come and go. Like putting on a sweater for the day, it can easily be pulled off. True self-confidence, or having a high estimation of yourself and your capabilities that is firmly rooted in the mind, is real inner self-confidence that is not easily shaken. It is not attached to your performance; it is attached to your being. It's more like a tattoo, something that cannot easily be removed.

When you develop your self-confidence, it is like planting a seedling that ultimately becomes a giant fruit tree: At first, the seedling needs watering, nurturing, and cultivation, enabling it to grow stronger and stronger every day and in every way. As it grows stronger, the tree eventually begins to flourish and bear fruit. The fruit becomes the visible sign and proof, or reward, of its existence and valor.

Low self-esteem can have a huge negative impact on a person's quality of life and trading. Low self-esteem can make you feel that you don't deserve the finer or better things in life or perhaps are not fit to enjoy and realize success. With low self-esteem and low self-worth, motivation levels can sink. Learning to trade may become self-defeating because you are always feeling low and being robbed of any enthusiasm.

Suffering from low self-esteem means you blame yourself for things that may not be your fault, such as the market not going your way. Many times we underestimate our abilities and expect things to go wrong for us. In other words, we expect to lose before we trade. Low self-esteem can position us to start thinking negatively about our trades before we even execute them and get our minds to start thinking of ways to subconsciously self-destruct or self-sabotage.

Often, low self-esteem is associated with a range of other problems, such as lack of confidence, depression, stress, or anxiety about your trading abilities. When you have low self-esteem, you may feel too embarrassed to ask important questions from mentors who can help you. You may not even want to communicate with the unseen but helpful individuals in online chat rooms, because you feel that your opinions and thoughts are worthless.

If that is the case, you will find yourself unable to connect or communicate effectively with others, which can become a real issue in learning how to become a successful trader. Frequently when we have low self-esteem, we find people who abuse us and we enter into abusive relationships. If you walk around with low self-esteem or are involved in some sort of abusive relationship, mentally or physically, then you are a perfect candidate to be abused by the market.

Lack of confidence will create negative emotions and will reflect in everything you do and say. It will affect your whole life. Traders who realize that they need help with confidence and self-esteem are often too embarrassed to admit to anyone that they have that type of problem. The majority of us live behind masks, and we fear exposure. Even though you may want to change the way you feel and be confident in your actions, your thoughts, or ideas you may have about trading, your subconscious mind knows differently. Even if you want to have a sense of faith in your own abilities and know consciously that you are worthwhile and respected, your emotional subconscious mind knows differently.

Confidence and Courage Lead to Success

Regardless of how badly you may want your success, if you have little or no confidence when you think about becoming a successful trader or being successful at anything, your mind goes back to your deepest insecurities, together with all the emotions held alongside those memories. All your subconscious beliefs surface to the top and are accessed. Your conscious mind, emotional mind, and subconscious mind are now in conflict. And after everything is said and done, the subconscious mind wins every time because your emotional mind will overrule the conscious mind. Your emotional mind will fight with your conscious mind. Your conscious mind will say, "You can be a winner, you are a winner," but your emotional mind will say, "OK, but what about this, and what about that? How could you have forgotten when you failed doing this and that?"

To succeed at trading, or anything for that matter, you must first believe that you *can*. The belief that you can puts you on the road to confidence. Your subconscious mind has the power to veto your emotional mind and end your struggle with your lack of confidence and low self-esteem. But it all begins with your belief system. If you think you are not a confident person, then you are right. If you think you are, yet deep inside you feel you are deceiving yourself, then you may be confident in one or two situations, but you will not maintain a confident demeanor, going back to the sweater analogy from earlier.

Habits of thought persist through our lives. While a healthy brain may reject a thought like "You really are confident," or perhaps a thought it really doesn't believe or no longer believes, the emotional side of the brain will continue to feel the same sentiments formerly associated with that belief. In other words, we can lie and deceive a lot of people, but deep inside we cannot lie and deceive ourselves.

The belief that we can puts us on the road to confidence.

When it comes to trading, you need to have the confidence to take chances. You need to be able to show others your real capabilities, instead of hiding them. If you are going to become a success at anything, even trading, you have to have the courage to address your feelings of fear, your feelings of inadequacy, and your feelings about the clutter and chaos in your life, enabling yourself to simply simplify.

Conclusion

Part of being a successful trader is acting like a successful trader. You have to learn how to win and not run away when you lose. Everyone has bad stretches and real successes. Either way, you have to be careful not to lose your confidence or become too confident. You need to trade with supreme confidence or you'll lose over and over again; then losing will become your new habit, which will end your trader's dream.

Your life will improve if you begin to believe in yourself and your abilities. You must have the courage to simplify your life and focus on the things that matter, like your belief that you were placed here on earth to achieve your highest potential. When we confront and overcome our fears and self-doubt and begin to believe we are destined for greatness, the world steps aside and allows us to achieve our goals and dreams. No one else can put that energy in motion. You must be responsible for your destiny and not place that burden on anyone else.

Your trading success will increase just from taking the action of believing that you are a successful trader. It will give you that extra boost to increase motivation, and your enthusiasm will increase every time you sit down to trade. Imagine how good it would feel to wake up morning after morning feeling in control, feeling strong, feeling free, and excited about your future at trading.

CHAPTER 15

PROTECT YOURSELF AT ALL TIMES

How many times have you been blindsided in life? Too often we take our emotional and physical safety for granted. We naively believe that our friends, family, boss, government, and even spouses or closest spiritual mentors will do us no harm, when in fact, they can be the biggest offenders and violators of our trust. Those we allow to get close to us leave us the most vulnerable and in some cases hurt us the most. We get involved in situations with people we trust, respect, and confide in, only to find out that in the end our trust and loyalty have been betrayed.

No one can be responsible or have control over the many bad things that happen to us in our lives, nor can we in most cases know how to prepare for such situations. There are no college courses we can take or degrees we can acquire on how to prepare for the awful, life-altering, unexpected bad events that will happen to us. All we can do as we are forced to work through those bad events that create such disappointments is control our own feelings and be responsible for our actions. Setbacks are a part of human existence; no one is immune. They can have dramatic adverse effects on us if we let them, but only *if* we let them. How we handle adversity in our lives is closely tied to the quality of our lives.

What is your programmed response when someone you don't know makes a mistake and places you in a position to believe you are now under attack? What is your programmed response when someone you do know, someone you love, makes a mistake and places you in a position to believe it is intentionally meant just to hurt you? When someone unconsciously cuts you off while driving, no doubt it can become a potential problem. But it was probably a human mistake on their part. It is how we subconsciously go about dealing with and resolving those types of problems, big or small, that determine our quality of life, daily peace, and personal happiness. When we choose to ineffectively solve our problems and act like a jerk—or, worse yet, like a psychopath—toward that innocent driver who made a human mistake or toward a store clerk, an operator, a waiter, our children, our partner, our boss, or whomever due to a sarcastic action or comment, we then rob ourselves of our peace and happiness and have not protected ourselves emotionally.

How we handle adversity in our lives is closely
tied to the quality of our lives.

When we do things in life that do not align with the natural laws of fairness, integrity, honesty, kindness, understanding, and forgiveness, then we are working against Karma and not protecting ourselves. We are not protecting our quality way of life that we get up every day for and set out to achieve. Rather, we slowly start to form negative and unwelcome habits that are counterproductive to our lives.

Protecting Yourself When Trading

You will take the habit of how you naturally or subconsciously respond to situations that frustrate or annoy you to the trading table. When it comes time to trade, and this market blindsides you or rapidly stops you out, what are you going to do? Are you going to try to pick an emotional fight with the market? If you do, you will lose just about every time. Negative actions in life are usually caused by negative emotions, and the market has plenty of room for both. When we allow negative emotions to take over and control our daily actions, we place ourselves in a position to incur a setback.

When you act before you think in the market, it can financially change your life forever. I have seen traders lose a lifetime of savings within hours after "picking a fight" with the market. You must realize you will never go through a season or year as an undefeated trader, because trading is not an undefeated game. You cannot win 100 percent of the time, but you can win the majority of the time. You cannot successfully make money 100 percent of the time, but you can acquire the habit of executing your trades 100 percent of the time according to your trading rules. And rule number one is: always protect yourself.

> Ask yourself, "If this trade does not go my way,
> can I live with the loss I will take?"

How do you protect yourself when trading? The first step is to properly educate yourself about how the market works and its potential risks. A surprising number of people think trading currencies is super risky. No doubt trading currencies involves risk, but a person's greatest risk in any type of trading is getting involved in something he or she knows nothing about. It is ignorance that creates risk. Think about it, if you were educated and taught where to get in the market and why, where to get out and why, and how to protect yourself, then where is the risk? It would be in the financial loss that you quantified *before* you executed the trade.

Protecting yourself in the marketplace means creating trading plans that you clearly understand, including one to make profit and one to indicate when to get out if the trade does not go your way. Quantify your potential downside first with every trading opportunity, knowing where you will get out if your trade does not go your way. In other words, trade with what is called a *protective stop-loss order*. A protective stop-loss order is an order placed at an area that quantifies a potential financial loss if the trade does not work out. Basically ask yourself, "If this trade does not go my way, can I live with the loss I will take? More important, will I have the ability financially and emotionally to trade again? Or will the loss be life altering?"

I have watched traders lose thousands of dollars, hundreds of thousands, even millions. When all was said and done, I asked them if it was worth it: 99.999 percent said no. They wish they would have thought through the downside of the trade and the repercussions financially and emotionally more carefully before they moved forward with it.

A friend of mine, being a mother of a four-year-old, would say, "Only pour as much milk in the cup as you can imagine being spilled." A large part of learning to become a successful trader is to do the following:

- Never trade without quantifying a potential loss first.
- Never trade without first looking at the downside, both emotionally and financially.
- Never trade without asking yourself, "If this trade does not work out, can I afford to lose the amount of money I am risking?"

In other words, never trade without a protective stop-loss order! In most cases, you may never know how much you can make in a trade. However, you surely can quantify how much you are willing to risk or lose before you trade.

Never trade without a protective stop-loss order!

Successful people don't believe that everything that shines is a diamond and everything that glitters is gold. They instead look at an opportunity for what it is. They are not driven by out-of-control emotional greed and are not tempted to act before properly planning.

As they do their due diligence and look at all their options and opportunities, their number one focus is to consider how much they will lose if this opportunity does not work out. They quantify a potential loss before they get involved, attaching a dollar amount and a deadline—whichever they hit first; they are disciplined enough to get out and walk away. When their idea or opportunity does not work within their timeline and prequalified investment, they don't keep going deeper in the red. They learn to financially protect themselves in everything they do, and it becomes a habit that serves them well during the course of their life.

Savvy investors look at capital preservation first. They say, "I know what I have; I don't know what I am going to get." They look at the potential risk, considering how much capital they will lose if things do not work out. They look at tax consequences second, and return on investment last. Ignorant or greedy investors look at return first and always say, "I am not worried about taxes; after all, this will work out and I will have plenty of money for taxes." They look at risk and capital preservation last. They are so sure the deal is going to pay off. But what happens in the end the majority of the time? They lose everything.

Protective Stop-Loss Orders in Life

In life, to experience the ultimate rewards of successful living, you need to learn how to create protective stop-loss orders for every opportunity found in business investments, business associates, friends, relatives, children, spouses, and every relationship. That discipline needs to become a habit.

Never risk more than you can afford to lose.

Many people have never considered a protective stop-loss order in managing their daily lives. However, it can become an incredible tool for helping you manage risk in everything you do: starting a business, running an existing business, hiring employees, dealing with coworkers, lending money to family and friends, and even managing your children and marriage. Protective stop losses can be seen as the creation of boundaries. In business we create financial boundaries, and in relationships we need to create emotional ones.

It is a known fact that approximately 95 percent of all new business start-ups end in failure within the first year. The main reason for such massive failures is due to the fact that most new business owners usually start without a business plan, jumping in because they get emotionally attached to an idea. When they begin to execute the emotional idea without a plan, they become emotionally attached to the opportunity. In the end, they are willing to do whatever it takes to survive and chase their emotional dream. When this 95 percent go bankrupt, it is not so much that their idea was not a good one, but mainly that they did not protect themselves by creating a business plan, clearly understanding their emotional and financial needs versus wants, and quantifying their protective stop-loss amount or order—that is, the place where they say, "This is all we are going to invest. When we get to that point, we are going to shut it down and look for another opportunity." Don't forget what happened to my friend in Chapter 3. He lost his house, his car, his life savings, even his marriage; his life was completely changed forever because he refused to first look at the downside of his investment. As for me and my family, because I quantified my loss before I invested, we managed to retain our quality of life even after losing my investment. Don't forget the number one rule: never risk more than you can afford to lose. Never risk so much that it will change your lifestyle or life forever.

Quantifying emotional stop losses are equally if not more important than financial stop-loss orders. It is about quantifying the amount of emotional heartache, abuse, or grief that you are willing to take should things not work out. It is drawing a line of tolerance in the sand, which allows us to manage the emotional risk levels with the perceived investment or relationship in our lives.

When we fail to properly protect ourselves, our quality of life can be altered or worse yet, we may get blindsided and incur a life-altering blow. The toll may be greater than we ever anticipated. It can affect our attitude, ego, emotions, financial security, marriage, and even destiny. One thing for certain is it will create an emotional scar that may take years to recover and heal from.

Four Simple Steps to Protecting Yourself

Turning the following four simple steps into daily habits can change your personal, financial, emotional, and trading life forever. These habits can participate in teaching you how to protect yourself with everything you do before you get involved.

1. **Look at what you have and ask, "How can I protect what I have from any loss or retain as much as I can if this opportunity does not work out?"** The first question while investing must always be, how can I preserve my initial investment should things go against me? The first question while entering into any relationship must always be, how can I preserve my existing relationship with this person should things start to get emotional between us? Believe it or not; emotional and personal relationship setbacks are usually greater than financial ones.

2. **Before you get involved, think through the worst situation that could arise if things do not work out as planned. Do not think of the best thing that can happen.** We all seem to naturally know how to act when everything is going great in our lives and in our relationships. It is when we have to work through the worst thing that could ever happen that we need to think through well and be very clear as to what we will do. Just as every building must have a fire exit, we need disaster plans in our lives to protect us.

3. **Create a plan that defines the terms and conditions of the opportunity.** If you fail to plan, you plan to fail. Every success is preceded with an executed well-thought-out, logical, and sound plan. When you make your plan, use the "if . . . then" approach. Successful people have plans in place that say, "If this happens, then I will do this," "If that happens, I will do

this," "If that doesn't happen, I will do this," and so on. Life is a game of chess with incredible variables. Trading has just as many. You need to be prepared for the unexpected surprises of life, and if you are prepared for the unexpected, then there are no unexpected surprises, only a continuation of your plan.

4. **Prove to yourself that your plan makes logical and financial sense and is the best thing for you and your loved ones.** Step back and ask yourself why you are getting involved. There are millions of opportunities in life and twice as many when it comes time to trading. When you learn to create a trading plan and follow it, you have a greater chance of success and really enjoying what you are doing. Your plans need to be logical-based, not emotion-based.

You are not protecting yourself if you take advantage of an opportunity without creating a sound plan with timelines, milestones, and stop losses along the way. Know when to get out when it is time to get out. You cannot afford to stay in the building when it is burning to the ground. When you begin to implement these four steps and allow them to become a part of your subconscious life, or a daily habit, before you get involved with anything or anyone, it will save you incredible amounts of money and years of grief in many areas of your life. When applied to trading, the habits will pay huge dividends when it is time to trade.

Personal Experience

I would like to share with you a very intimate personal experience that I touched on briefly in an earlier chapter. I feel compelled to give you the detailed version of what happened, in the spirit of having my bad past judgment help you develop good judgment in the future and help you avoid a lot of emotional pain as well as financial loss.

I will never forget the time I lost a year's worth of income in less than 5 hours. It was a beautiful Friday morning, and my wife and I wanted to go to the beach and spend the weekend with our children. So I said to my wife, "Honey, I'll make you a deal, if you get ready with the kids and pack the car, I will make a couple of trades by noon that will make us a few thousand dollars and enable us to really enjoy our weekend." She said, "Deal."

After breakfast I sat down at my computer, being used to trading the U.S. session, and all of a sudden I saw a setup. I entered the market with 30K to 100K lots that pay $10 a pips per lot (which is $300 for every pip the market moves, or $3,000 for every 10 pips in movement). All I wanted was about 30 pips to enjoy my weekend. After I got in the market, the market began to move in my direction. But to my surprise, it missed my limit order by 3 pips, came all the way back to my entry, and then went the opposite way about 25 pips. I thought to myself, "I wonder what is going on here. I was up around $7,500, and now I am down about $7,500."

At the time, I was getting use to my new name FXCHIEF, and out of a false sense of security due to my title, I was committing the ultimate trader's sin that I always teach and preach against: trading without a protective stop. I thought, "I'm the Chief, and I have everything under control."

Looking at the movement of the charts I thought, "No problem, the market is obviously going sideways, so I will buy another 30 lots at this level of support the market is making and take the ride up to resistance." In the stock market this approach is used when the market slightly corrects itself, and I figured I would use that same trick of "cost averaging down" that wiped out all the mutual and stock funds during all the major stock market corrections. This is an ignorant trick, and as the saying goes, the ignorant must suffer! That single trading trick was responsible for the many failures of stock funds in the stock market when it not only plummeted, but corrected 10 years of up price movement with in a matter of months . . . but I used it anyhow.

With now being in the market with 60K to 100K lots, I was making and losing $600 a pip. All I wanted was the market to move back in my favor by 10 pips, and I would make $6,000. Now that I had cost averaged down and entered at two different locations on the two sets of 30 lot increments, the market really needed to get to my breakeven to start making $600 a pip. When the market came to my breakeven, it shot back down again in the opposite direction, and in no time I was now down about $30,000. I thought, "No worries, I am the FXCHIEF, I have everything under control" and entered the market with another 30 lots. I was now 90 lots in a trade that is $900 a pip again at above a breakeven and $900 a pip in losses below my entry on my third set of lots. As I sat there, a little nervous and confident at the same time, it started to move in my direction, bringing me some emotional relief but very little financial relief. All I knew was I was in the market without a trading plan or any quantified protective stop-loss orders! All of a sudden, the market shot down further, like an airplane falling out of the sky. Within a few minutes, I was $200,000 in the red and now very concerned.

As the saying goes, desperate people do desperate things, and I was about to do the most desperate act a trader can do: risk it all. As the market kept moving against me, I tried to figure out the average daily trading range. I said, "I am going to show this market how smart I am and how well I know what it does and that I am not wrong. *I am the FXCHIEF!* As it started to bottom out around 1:00 p.m. EST after the European session had closed, I entered with another 30 lots. At this point I was up to 120 lots—$1,200 per pip movement after breakeven and $1,200 a pip moving against me, or $12,000 every 10 pips.

It doesn't take long for the ocean to drown someone in a storm, and it doesn't take long for the market to drown someone financially, teach them a lesson in respect and humility. By 2:00 p.m. in the afternoon, knowing the markets close at 4:00 p.m. on Friday, I had worked my way down on my knees shaking, trembling, and even somewhat crying, mainly because shortly after I entered with my last set of lots, the market dipped even further and I was down about $350,000 in five hours. Now I was pleading and crying to God for help, promising that if He will just help me out, if He would just get me out of this trade at breakeven, hell, even at a $30,000 or $50,000 loss, I would *never* trade again without a protective stop-loss order *ever again*, I meant *never*. I even committed to go to church and pay 20 percent in my gains in tithes instead of the typical 10 percent, if He would just get me out of this trade. What was amazing is the more the market moved against me and the greater my pain, the greater the percentage I was willing to give. I remember thinking, hell, God take it all, you decide what you want and make the market come back to what you want, because if you can get me out of this, you can have it all. Desperate people do desperate and sometimes offensive things.

> It doesn't take long for the ocean to drown someone in a storm, and it doesn't take long for the market to drown someone financially.

Life is nothing but a comedy for those who think their way through it and a real tragedy for those who feel their way through it. I was now unable to think, as my left brain had shut down. I could only use my right brain and feel, and I was feeling sick. I was in a total stupor, just like a deer looking at oncoming headlights. I was in a state of shock, fear, anger, frustration, and ultimate sorrow. I was thinking that every trader should be forced to trade in an low-volt electric chair so when they break a little rule, the shock will teach them and they will never allow themselves to break any of the big rules (like trading without a stop-loss order). Breaking some rules at trading can be like traveling through downtown New York ignoring all red lights; face it, you *will* get hit! But trading without a protective stop loss is more like jumping off the Brooklyn Bridge.

When we make mistakes or when things go wrong, we have a tendency to try to blame others for our misfortune or pain. The reality in this situation was there was no one to blame but me, my own greedy stupidity and perhaps my ego—after all I was the FXCHIEF now in FX disbelief.

In the heat of battle, I called a friend for help, a successful Forex trader who was somewhat of a mentor for me. After I told him what was going on and what I did, he said, "The first thing I want you to do is to get off your knees." I said, "How do you know I am on my knees?" He responded, "Anyone who makes it at trading has spent a great amount of time on their knees in prayer!"

Now let me show you how powerful fear and greed are in our lives and in the market. After speaking with him and basically subjecting myself to his logical mercy, as my brain was emotionally fried, all of a sudden, the market began to make a U-turn and rally back to my entries. Within 30 minutes the market came all the way back, and my account went from being over $350,000 in the red to now showing a $9,000 profit—the original amount I wanted to make to enjoy my weekend.

As the market raced back, my friend said, "You are the luckiest SOB I have ever met!" Then he yelled, "Get out, now!" I screamed back, "Are you crazy? I am not getting out now. This thing is going to come all the way back and pay me $350,000." Now you must remember I have just returned from the depths of hell, submerged in fear, pain, grief, and sorrow. Still being in a state of shock, I was so blinded to reality that not only did I think I got out of hell, but I thought I was on a flight to paradise.

Within minutes after negotiating with God and begging God to deal graciously with me, I found myself so filled with greed, wanting more and more, completely forgetting my commitments. I became so completely emotionally blind, I didn't know what I was doing. My emotions were now in total control of my actions, and logic no longer played a part.

After I told my friend I was not getting out, he yelled back, "You are the dumbest idiot I know! God gave you a break, and now you make a mockery of it. You deserve to lose it all!" and hung up the phone.

Well, as fate had it, within 15 minutes his "death wish" became my "reality." Just as fast as the market rallied back to my advantage, it whiplashed back the other way, and I was liquidated. Let me repeat this: *Sorrow is such a determined teacher; what I once did, I shall never do again.*

Was it worth it? Absolutely not! We do not have to go through life running red lights and being T-boned trying to survive being in a critical condition to learn our lessons of how to protect ourselves.

Conclusion

Clever is he who learns from his own mistakes; wise is he who learns from the mistakes of others. Learn from my mistakes. Learn how to protect yourself in every trade. Whenever you get involved with anything, look at the downside first. Protect yourself first. Don't underestimate the power of Murphy's law: if anything can go wrong, it will go wrong. (Murphy lives in the market and in our computers when we are trading.)

Move forward hoping for the best but also protecting yourself as if the worst were to happen. Create a disaster plan before you execute the plan; then when the disaster happens, it is not a disaster. It will then have been part of the plan. Every great building has several fire exits. Create your fire exits first in everything you do. What good is the beauty and strength of a building if you die in the fire? Always protect yourself!

FOLLOW YOUR DREAMS AND PERSIST UNTIL YOU SUCCEED

Now we come to the final chapter where we can reflect and ask a simple, though important, question: "Can any of the information in this book really help me create a dream, continue with my dream, or improve my life?" I certainly believe so, as the mindset presented in these past 15 chapters has helped lead not only to my financial success, but to happiness and achievements in all areas of my life.

One of my greatest pleasures in life has been doing what people say I cannot do. When someone tries to steal your dream and tells you that you can't do something, don't quit—just smile and say, "I'll show you." If you don't chase your dream, if you don't go after what you want, you'll never get it. You are braver than you believe, stronger than you seem, and smarter than you think. Don't let people take your dreams away from you. All of us dream to live a life of happiness and abundance, achieving our highest potential, so why not live that dream? The future belongs to those who believe in the beauty of their dreams and in the power and passion they bring to them.

Market Traders Institute (MTI) exists today because after I learned to trade, I knew what other people were going to be up against. I also knew that in homes across the world, there would be fathers and mothers that this market would scare to death, beat up, demoralize, humiliate, and rob their dignity as people.

I understand how scary, challenging, and awful it can be to chase the dream of becoming a trader. I lived through the difficulties, the horror, the trying and embarrassing moments, including times when I did not even have enough money to buy new shoes for my kids. No doubt I had a lot of resentments, fears, and doubts as I was working through my trading problems.

When I was learning to trade, I thought about trading as I ate, drank, and slept. It consumed my life. I learned to never give up on something that you can't go a day without thinking about. But I had to face the hard-core reality that I had to figure things out on my own if I wanted to survive and succeed at this. I was forced to have a strong *will* instead of a strong *won't*. My having chosen a mindset of looking at my problems as potential opportunities or ways to try again more intelligently has allowed me to plow through my problems and create a quality way of life for me and my family. What I have accomplished has done wonders for my self-worth, self-confidence, and self-esteem. I have already shared with you how humiliated and beat-up I felt as I was learning how to trade. If learning to trade has done all this for me, it will do wonders for you!

Do not take lightly what you have read in this book. This mindset and trader's life have come to me at a price, but a price that I was willing to pay to chase my dream. I have always tried to counterattack problems I faced with a positive attitude and optimistic outlook. Still to this day I attempt to find solutions that enable me to move problems out of the way without blame or causing additional ones. Of course, I know there is always a new set of problems anxiously waiting to surface, and dealing with too many at one time can be overwhelming. So I handle each one as it comes, always keeping my ultimate goals in mind.

Traders who have a subconscious daily habit of not dealing with their problems or need to get back at people rather than address the problem are doomed at trading. We take our habits with us everywhere we go, especially when trading. Bringing in such bad habits or pessimistic thoughts, however, will stop you from succeeding in the market.

Successful living and successful trading are all about finding a remedy, not faults. Don't get hung up on finding fault; stay focused on finding closure and on what to do next. Spend your energies on moving forward toward the answer that will eliminate your problem and turn things around for you.

After teaching thousands of people around the globe how to trade, I would have to say the one personal characteristic that I would regard as being the most important trait necessary to succeed not only in life but also as a trader is *persistence*. It is that sheer determination to endure to the end after getting knocked down 100 times and then getting back up 101 times with a positive attitude, saying, "Here comes number 101, like it or not!" Persist until you succeed.

When you get to a point where you think this whole market—everything and everyone involved in it—is against you and you adamantly feel you cannot hang on, not even for one minute longer, it is right then and there that you cannot give up. For that is just the place and time when everything is going to turn around. That is your "trader's moment of truth." The trader who can persist a little longer once the effort is painful is the one who will ultimately find success. As long as we are persistent in the pursuit of our trading dreams, we will continue to grow.

I think a truly successful trader is an ordinary person who finds the strength to persist, persevere, and endure in spite of all the overwhelming obstacles and odds he or she will face in the market. Nothing in this world can take the place of persistence.

However, reasonable traders do not fight the market; rather they adapt themselves to the market and persist until they succeed. Unreasonable traders persist and demand that the market adapt to their world. That is where a problem lies. You cannot insist that this market adapt to your needs. It will not happen.

Persistence allows you to get back on track when you hit a detour. It allows you to reevaluate and readjust your way of thinking as you reapproach the market. There are traders who persisted until they succeeded. They finally figured it out. Nonetheless, they were confronted with additional problems, which they would not believe were dead-ends. They had the insight and courage to call them challenges. Challenges and obstacles are put in our way to see if what we want is really what we want and if it is worth fighting for.

Great lives are created by ordinary people like you and me who have the courage to think great thoughts and follow up with great actions. To accomplish great things, we must not only act, but also dream; we must not only plan, but also believe. You have to believe you are capable of succeeding at anything you do in life, especially at trading—otherwise, you will give up! It's not because things are difficult that we don't try. It is because we do not try the things that we believe are difficult. Nothing great has ever been achieved except by those who truly believed that something inside them was greater than the obstacle or problem. Your big opportunity may be right where you are now. It may be in trading on the Forex.

Nobody is a natural at trading. When it comes to trading, you become good by working hard, and you get better by practicing over and over a trading technique that you understand. Success will come by not trying to do everything. You must keep it simple. *Do not* complicate it. When you make a mistake, remember what doesn't destroy you will only make you a stronger and wiser trader.

Dare to be successful in life and at trading. Persist until you succeed and *never forget*: in the confrontation between the stream and the rock, the stream always wins—not through strength, but through pure persistence. Look at the Grand Canyon!

INDEX